From the Pages of
The Communist Manifesto
and Other Writings

A specter is haunting Europe—the specter of Communism.
(from *Manifesto of the Communist Party*, page 5)

The history of all hitherto existing society is the history of class struggles.
(from *Manifesto of the Communist Party*, page 7)

Society as a whole is splitting up more and more into two great hostile camps, into two great classes directly facing each other: Bourgeoisie and Proletariat.
(from *Manifesto of the Communist Party*, page 8)

The bourgeoisie during its rule of scarce one hundred years has created more massive and more colossal productive forces than have all preceding generations together. Subjection of nature's forces to man, machinery, application of chemistry to industry and agriculture, steam navigation, railways, electric telegraphs, clearing of whole continents for cultivation, canalization of rivers, whole populations conjured out of the ground— what earlier century had even a presentiment that such productive forces slumbered in the lap of social labor?
(from *Manifesto of the Communist Party*, page 12)

Modern industry has converted the little workshop of the patriarchal master into the great factory of the industrial capitalist. Masses of laborers, crowded into the factory, are organized like soldiers. As privates of the industrial army they are placed under the command of a perfect hierarchy of officers and sergeants. Not only are they slaves of the bourgeois class and of the bourgeois State; they are daily and hourly enslaved by the machine, by the overseer and, above all, by the individual bourgeois manufacturer himself. The more openly this despotism proclaims gain to be its end and aim, the more petty, the more hateful and the more embittering it is.
(from *Manifesto of the Communist Party*, page 14)

The theory of the Communists may be summed up in the single sentence: Abolition of private property.
(from *Manifesto of the Communist Party*, page 21)

The Communists disdain to conceal their views and aims. They openly declare that their ends can be attained only by the forcible overthrow of all existing social conditions. Let the ruling classes tremble at a Communistic revolution. The proletarians have nothing to lose but their chains. They have a world to win.   (from *Manifesto of the Communist Party*, page 41)

WORKING MEN OF ALL COUNTRIES, UNITE!
(from *Manifesto of the Communist Party*, page 41)

Hegel remarks somewhere that all facts and personages of great importance in world history occur, as it were, twice. He forgot to add: the first time as tragedy, the second as farce.
(from *The Eighteenth Brumaire of Louis Bonaparte*, page 63)

The social revolution of the nineteenth century cannot draw its poetry from the past, but only from the future.
(from *The Eighteenth Brumaire of Louis Bonaparte*, page 66)

In the first French Revolution the rule of the *Constitutionalists* is followed by the rule of the *Girondists* and the rule of the *Girondists* by the rule of the *Jacobins*. Each of these parties relies on the more progressive party for support. As soon as it has brought the revolution far enough to be unable to follow it further, still less to go ahead of it, it is thrust aside by the bolder ally that stands behind it and sent to the guillotine. The revolution thus moves along an ascending line.
(from *The Eighteenth Brumaire of Louis Bonaparte*, page 87)

By now stigmatizing as "*socialistic*" what it had previously extolled as "*liberal*," the bourgeoisie confesses that its own interests dictate that it should be delivered from the danger of its *own rule*.
(from *The Eighteenth Brumaire of Louis Bonaparte*, page 108)

This extra-parliamentary bourgeoisie, which had already rebelled against the purely parliamentary and literary struggle for the rule of its own class and betrayed the leaders of this struggle, now dares after the event to indict the proletariat for not having risen in a bloody struggle, a life-and-death struggle on its behalf!   (from *The Eighteenth Brumaire of Louis Bonaparte*, page 143)

If ever an event has, well in advance of its coming, cast its shadow before, it was Bonaparte's *coup d'état*.
(from *The Eighteenth Brumaire of Louis Bonaparte*, pages 146–147)

The revolution is thoroughgoing. It is still journeying through purgatory. It does its work methodically.
(from *The Eighteenth Brumaire of Louis Bonaparte*, page 156)

THE COMMUNIST MANIFESTO

AND OTHER WRITINGS

Karl Marx and Friedrich Engels

*With an Introduction and Notes
by Martin Puchner*

George Stade
Consulting Editorial Director

JB
BARNES & NOBLE CLASSICS
NEW YORK

JB

BARNES & NOBLE CLASSICS

NEW YORK

Published by Barnes & Noble Books
122 Fifth Avenue
New York, NY 10011

www.barnesandnoble.com/classics

Manifesto of the Communist Party was first published in German in 1848. The text of the present edition is that of the 1888 English edition, which was minimally edited and revised by Friedrich Engels.

Originally published in trade paperback format by Barnes & Noble Classics with new Introduction, Notes, Biography, Chronology, Inspired By, Comments & Questions, and For Further Reading. This hardcover edition published in 2005.

The Communist Manifesto and Other Writings
ISBN-13: 978-1-59308-375-5
ISBN-10: 1-59308-375-0
LC Control Number 2005931406

Produced and published in conjunction with:
Fine Creative Media, Inc.
322 Eighth Avenue
New York, NY 10001

Michael J. Fine, President and Publisher

Printed in the United States of America

1 3 5 7 9 10 8 6 4 2

FIRST PRINTING

Karl Marx

Philosopher, historian, economist, social scientist, and revolutionary, Karl Marx was born on May 5, 1818, in Trier, Prussia (now Germany). His family were middle-class Jews who had converted to Lutheranism; Karl's father expected his son, who was gifted in many subjects, to follow in his footsteps and become a lawyer. But when his father sent Karl to study law in Bonn, the young man preferred to carouse, smoke, compose poetry, and fall in love. After becoming engaged to Jenny von Westphalen, Marx transferred to the law faculty of the University of Berlin, though the degree he eventually earned was a doctorate in philosophy.

Marx turned to journalism to earn his living. The fiery polemicist edited and wrote for the liberal newspaper *Rheinische Zeitung*, his deeply critical articles provoked the ire of the Prussian government, which dissolved the paper in 1843. Karl and Jenny then married and moved to Paris. Marx studied political economy and French socialism that year and, as a result, became a communist, though he was still working out the precise tenets of that political philosophy. His legendary intellect roused much support, but his revolutionary writings resulted in his expulsion by the French government, later by the Belgian government, and eventually by Prussia, his native country. England was the last outpost for Marx, and he lived there, working tirelessly on behalf of workers, until the end of his life.

Despite the fact that he suffered periods of poor health and poverty, Marx created an extremely influential body of thought. He mastered many foreign languages and spent years in the library, learning philosophy, history, and economics. His writings helped change the way the world views the relationship between labor and capital, and his works, foremost among them *The Communist Manifesto* and *Capital*, are widely read to this day. Karl Marx died in London on March 14, 1883.

Friedrich Engels

Remembered as Karl Marx's collaborator and the co-founder of communism, Friedrich Engels was born on November 28, 1820, in Barmen, Prussia (now Wuppertal, Germany). His father, a wealthy textile manufacturer, groomed his son for a career in the family trade. Young Friedrich fulfilled this obligation, but not without nurturing his own intellectual and political interests. He spent many years at the family's Manchester factory, where he observed capitalism firsthand, observations that no doubt affected his important work *The Condition of the Working Class in England.*

The family business allowed Engels to support the impoverished Marx family. Together, Engels and Marx organized revolutionary groups of workers in France, Germany, and Belgium. They also produced the famous *The Communist Manifesto* and developed their ideas on historical materialism in *The German Ideology.* Many underestimate Engels's contributions to the partnership, but works like his *Anti-Dühring* (a defense of Marx), and others, enjoyed great popularity in their time, and it was only through Engels's dedicated labor that Marx's unfinished works, including the last two volumes of *Capital,* were published. Friedrich Engels died on August 5, 1895, in London.

Table of Contents

The World of Karl Marx, Friedrich Engels,
and The Communist Manifesto
ix

Introduction by Martin Puchner
xiii

THE COMMUNIST MANIFESTO
AND OTHER WRITINGS
1

Manifesto of the Communist Party *[1848, 1888]*
3

Prefaces to the Manifesto of the Communist Party
[1872–1893]
43

The Eighteenth Brumaire of Louis Bonaparte *[1852]*
61

Prefaces to The Eighteenth Brumaire of Louis Bonaparte
[1869, 1885]
171

Theses on Feuerbach *[1845/46, 1888]*
177

Comments & Questions
183

For Further Reading
189

The World of Karl Marx, *Friedrich Engels, and* The Communist Manifesto

1818   Karl Marx is born on May 5 to Heinrich and Henriette Marx in Trier, Prussia (now Germany). His father, a lawyer who had converted from Judaism to Lutheranism in order to be allowed to practice his profession in the Prussian Empire, expects Karl to become an attorney as well.

1820   Friedrich Engels is born on November 28 in Barmen, Prussia (now Wuppertal, Germany), to a wealthy textile manufacturer with interests in both Barmen and Manchester, England. Friedrich's father grooms him from an early age to join the family business.

1835   Marx enters Bonn University as a law student. To his father's dismay, the young man is more interested in writing poetry, falling in love, and drinking and smoking late into the night with his friends.

1836   During the summer, Marx becomes engaged to Jenny von Westphalen, a beautiful girl from a respected Trier family. In October, Marx transfers to Berlin University to study first law, then philosophy; he joins the Young Hegelian Doctors' Club.

1837   Engels leaves school to join the family textile business.

1838   Engels goes to Bremen for business training; he also writes for the press.

1841   Marx is awarded his doctorate. Engels returns home to Barmen but soon enlists in the military for a one-year term and goes to Berlin, where he attends lectures in his free time and joins the Young Hegelians.

1842   Marx begins contributing to the liberal newspaper *Rheinische Zeitung*, published in Cologne. His first article carries the headline "Comments on the Latest Prussian Censorship Instruction." In October, Marx is named editor of the newspaper. Engels contributes to the paper on a number of political and social issues. Engels travels to Manchester, England, to work in the family's factory there. Marx and Engels meet for the first time in November, in the *Rheinische Zeitung* office in Cologne.

1843   Because of Marx's radical critiques of its policies, the Prussian government orders the closing of *Rheinische Zeitung*. Marx and Jenny marry and move to Paris.

1844   Marx and Jenny's first child, Jenny, is born. Engels contributes two articles to the *Deutsche-Französische Jahrbücher* (*German-French Yearbook*), which Marx is editing. Engels visits Marx in Paris in September; they begin their first joint work, *Die Heilige Familie* (*The Holy Family*), a critique of the Young Hegelians.

1845   Under pressure from Prussia, the French government ousts Marx for his revolutionary activities. Marx moves to Brussels. In the spring, he writes *Theses on Feuerbach*. Engels soon joins him there, and the two men work on *The German Ideology*, which contains their ideas on historical materialism. Engels publishes *Lage der Arbeitenden Klasse in England* (*The Condition of the Working Class in England*). Marx and Engels go to England to study new English works on economics. In London, they meet with the leaders of the Chartists. Marx and Jenny's second daughter, Laura, is born.

1847   Karl and Jenny Marx's son Edgar is born. Marx and Engels accept a proposal from the London committee of the League of the Just to help it reorganize and write its new agenda; later in the year the organization changes its name to the Communist League. Marx and Engels help found a German Workers' Society in Brussels; most members are working-class German refugees. Marx publishes *Misère de la Philosophie* (*The Poverty of Philosophy*), which attacks the socialist ideas of Pierre-Joseph Proudhon.

1848   *Manifest der Kommunistischen Partei* (*The Communist Manifesto*) is published, and Marx is expelled from Belgium. Revolutions occur throughout Europe. Marx and Engels return to

Cologne and in June start a daily newspaper, *Neue Rheinische Zeitung*.

1849 After a counter-revolution in Prussia, Marx and Engels, as editors of *Neue Rheinische Zeitung*, are tried for insulting the authorities; a jury finds them not guilty, but soon afterward the government orders Marx to leave the country. He goes to Paris but is soon expelled by the authorities. He seeks asylum in London, where his fourth child, Heinrich, is born in November. Engels arrives in London a few days later. Marx spends many hours in the library of the British Museum, researching and writing articles and essays.

1850 Marx's *Die Klassenkampfe in Frankreich, 1848 bis 1850 (The Class Struggles in France, 1848–1850)* is published. The infant Heinrich Marx dies. Engels takes a job in the family firm in Manchester and begins financially supporting Marx.

1851 Franziska Marx, a daughter, is born to Karl and Jenny Marx.

1852 Franziska Marx dies. *The Eighteenth Brumaire of Louis Bonaparte* is published in New York.

1855 Marx and Jenny's daughter Eleanor is born in January; in April, their son Edgar dies.

1857 Marx begins work on his *Grundrisse der Kritik der Politischen Ökonomie (Fundamentals of a Critique of Political Economy)*, a series of notebooks aimed at pulling together all his theoretical economic ideas; they will not be published until the next century.

1859 Marx's *Zur Kritik der Politischen Ökonomie (Contribution to the Critique of Political Economy)* is published.

1864 The International Workingmen's Association (the First International) is founded in London; Marx is elected a member of its Provisional Committee and drafts both the Provisional Rules and the Inaugural Address.

1867 The first volume of *Das Kapital (Capital)* is published. Engels publishes a brief biography of Marx.

1869 Engels sells his partnership in the family business and retires. Marx learns Russian in order to study Russian economic writings.

1870 Marx is invited to become corresponding secretary of the General Council for Russia, part of the First International.

Engels moves from Manchester to London; he is elected to the General Council of the First International and made corresponding secretary for Belgium, Italy, Spain, Portugal, and Denmark.

1871   Marx writes and publishes *The Civil War in France.*

1872   Marx and Engels participate in the London Congress of the First International.

1877   Engels begins serializing *Anti-Dühring,* a response to the ideas of Eugen Dühring, a critic of Marx; it will be published in book form the following year, in Leipzig. Marx corresponds with radicals throughout the United States and Europe.

1881   Marx's wife, Jenny, dies, leaving him devastated.

1883   Marx's eldest daughter, Jenny, dies in January. Marx dies in his armchair in London on March 14. Although only eleven people attend Marx's funeral in Highgate Cemetery, Engels's eulogy will prove true: "In every single field which Marx investigated . . . he made independent discoveries. . . . His name will endure through the ages, and so also will his work!"

1884   Engels publishes a monograph, *Der Ursprung der Familie, des Privateigenthums und des Staats* (*The Origin of the Family, Private Property, and the State*). Throughout the remaining years of his life, Engels will edit the voluminous body of unpublished work Marx left behind at his death, including volumes two and three of *Capital,* published in 1885 and 1894, respectively.

1888   Engels publishes *Ludwig Feuerbach and the Outcome of Classical German Philosophy.*

1889   Engels participates in the founding of the Second International.

1895   Engels dies in London on August 5, 1895.

Introduction

Written within less than five years of each other, *The Communist Manifesto* (1848) and *The Eighteenth Brumaire of Louis Bonaparte* (1852) are the bookends to the most revolutionary period of the nineteenth century. With the exception of Great Britain, most countries in western and central Europe experienced some kind of revolutionary upheaval around the year 1848. (Two generations earlier, the French Revolution had broken the old aristocratic order in France, but the effects of that revolution had been contained by the restoration of the monarchy in 1814.) Now, Europe's disenfranchised classes—the peasants, parts of the bourgeoisie, and the proletariat—once more articulated their demands through strikes, mass demonstrations, and acts of resistance. This was the context in which Karl Marx and Friedrich Engels composed the *Manifest der Kommunistischen Partei* (*Manifesto of the Communist Party*, mostly known as *The Communist Manifesto*) in 1847. It was published in London in February 1848, only weeks before the outbreak of the first phase of the 1848 revolution in France, the so-called February Revolution. The primary purpose of the *Manifesto* was to announce and publicize that the communists had given up on the conspiratorial activities of the past and were now entering the scene of politics through an open declaration of principle. The preamble states this goal unequivocally: "It is high time that Communists should openly, in the face of the whole world, publish their views, their aims, their tendencies, and meet this nursery tale of the Specter of Communism with a Manifesto of the party itself" (p. 5). Instead of being confined to secret societies and intrigues, communism had acquired a public face.

Even though the publication of the *Manifesto* had no material impact on France's February Revolution, its enthusiastic tone makes it clear that it was written in anticipation of a social revolution that it perceived to be imminent. The two authors knew that such a revolution would encounter opposition from those intent on preserving the status quo, but they had seen the proletariat grow stronger and more self-confident by the day and therefore hoped that once united, it would be capable of breaking its chains. The famous first sentence speaks of communism as a "specter" that is haunting Europe. But the *Manifesto* is certain that communism is about to cease being a mere specter and start becoming the real thing.

If the *Manifesto* is overly confident with regard to the incipient revolution, *Der Achtzehnte Brumaire des Louis Bonaparte* (*The Eighteenth Brumaire of Louis Bonaparte*) is the analysis of its failure. Following his earlier call for action, Marx issued a call for analysis. It was an analysis born out of disappointment. The text was commissioned by a German publisher in New York City asking Marx to explain what went wrong in France, why the revolution had, within the course of a few years, gradually lost ground only to be entirely undone by the coup d'état of Louis Bonaparte, a figure who had hitherto attracted only ridicule. Marx did not content himself with poking fun at Louis Bonaparte, his hapless policies and inarticulate pronouncements. Rather, he sought to explain the root causes for the initial success and the eventual failure of the revolution. The result is a brilliant example of social analysis, bringing into relation the values and interests of different groups and classes, their policies, shifting alliances, mistakes, and lies. While the *Manifesto* is a text for times of revolutionary upheaval, the *Eighteenth Brumaire* is a text for times of reaction.

The *Manifesto* and the *Eighteenth Brumaire* were thus intimately tied to one event, the Revolution of 1848. At the same time, they both radiated far beyond this original context. The *Manifesto*, in particular, became an international success story, one of the texts that influenced world history more directly and lastingly than most. Few texts have been translated into more languages and been printed in more editions, few have inspired more fear and hope than this one, whose significance puts it on a par with foundational texts such as the Bible and the Koran. The *Manifesto* was read, translated, adopted, transformed, updated, and critiqued by politicians and activists, by scholars and organizers around the world. But the *Eighteenth Brumaire*, too, has left its mark. When revolutionary hopes inspired by texts modeled on the *Manifesto* waned, disappointed activists turned to this latter work for guidance and inspiration, and then modeled their own analyses of failed revolutions on the failure of the revolution of 1848.

Despite the undeniable influence and success of both texts, the question remains how we should read them today, in the first decade of the twenty-first century, and after the fall of most socialist regimes in 1989. It has been tempting to assume that with the fall of socialism in the late twentieth century, the writer who inspired socialism has fallen as well. The two texts written around 1848 thus seem to be proven wrong by the events that took place 141 years later. Even though such a historical conclusion is ultimately misguided, the two texts collected here are nevertheless intertwined with the history of socialism in the twentieth century. Indeed, the *Manifesto*'s influence on the Bolshevik Revolution of 1917, and the establishment of a socialist society in the Soviet Union and elsewhere, helped this text acquire its status of world historical importance, even though it said little about the transition from a socialist society to a truly communist one, in which private property, and the state, would have withered away. And it was in the Soviet Union that the *Manifesto* was studied most systematically, printed and reprinted, and integrated into the official discipline called Marxism-Leninism. But while the Bolshevik Revolution helped the *Manifesto* gain its significance, it also limited the ways in which it was read and interpreted. Neither the *Manifesto* nor the *Eighteenth Brumaire* were written to justify the particular form of social, economic, or political organization established in the Soviet Union, nor indeed any other type of state. For this reason, the fact that history has swept away these regimes opens these texts, and all of Marx's writings, to new readings—readings that can help in our understanding of our own moment in history.

Perhaps the *Manifesto* is most relevant to us today in terms of what we call globalization. Some of Marx's most passionate paragraphs describe what he identified, more than 150 years ago, as a process by which national independence was giving way to interdependence, an internationalism brought about by the immense unleashing of productive forces through capitalism. It is important to recognize here that Marx was not simply hostile to capitalism and its globalizing effects. Indeed, he credits the bourgeoisie, the capitalist class as such, with an immensely revolutionary role in history, one that did away with older feudal relations. And just as bourgeois capitalism destroyed feudalism, so it destroyed national autonomy and created instead a world market characterized by an increasingly frenzied exchange of natural resources, products, and populations. Here is one of the most gripping paragraphs of the *Manifesto*:

> The bourgeoisie has through its exploitation of the world market given a cosmopolitan character to production and consumption in every country. To the great chagrin of Reactionists, it has drawn from under the feet of industry the national ground on which it stood. All old-established national industries have been destroyed or are daily being destroyed. They are dislodged by new industries, whose introduction becomes a life and death question for all civilized nations, by industries that no longer work up indigenous raw material but raw material drawn from the remotest zones; industries whose products are consumed, not only at home, but in every quarter of the globe. In place of the old wants, satisfied by the production of the country, we find new wants, requiring for their satisfaction the products of distant lands and climes. In place of the old local and national seclusion and self-sufficiency, we have intercourse in every direction, universal interdependence of nations. And as in material, so also in intellectual production. The intellectual creations of individual nations become common property. National one-sidedness and narrow-mindedness become more and more impossible, and from the numerous national and local literatures there arises a world literature (pp. 10–11).

At a time such as the present, when some groups agitating against global capitalism call for a return to older, more local forms of living, it is worth remembering the example of Marx, who attacked the injustices created by the world market by calling not for an end to globalization but rather for its transformation.

In reaction to a brutal and destructive global capitalism, which left whole populations impoverished, land devastated, and once-flourishing ecologies destroyed, Marx demanded a new internationalism that would not try to turn back the wheel of history but rather seize it and steer it into a new and better direction. Marx's answer, the creation of a socialist international organization that would not only coordinate the different national socialist parties but also become the unified organ of the international proletariat, proved in the end ineffective. The First International soon gave way to the so-called Second International, which lasted until World War I, after which point the Third International was born; it lasted until World War II. During the Cold War, the internationalist rhetoric of socialism was replaced by the creation of the Cominform (the Communist Information Bureau; established in 1947 to promote international communist solidarity, it became a Soviet propaganda mechanism), though Leon Trotsky had founded an alternative Fourth International, independent from Moscow, in the 1930s. The era of the Internationals has now ended. What still remains is the task of responding to the increasing interdependence of nations with a new internationalism, of addressing everything from ecological crises and natural catastrophes to humanitarian crises in a responsible, and therefore international, manner. What we can learn from Marx today is that we need not react to the violence of globalization with a call for a return to a state before globalization. We might instead call for a new and different form of globalization, an internationalism driven not by the putatively natural laws of the market but by the responsible actions of humans.

The internationalism of the *Manifesto* was also due to Marx's own experience, his life of exile. After studying philosophy and writing a dissertation on pre-Socratic philosophy, Marx became increasingly politicized and involved with a radical newspaper called *Rheinische Zeitung*, based in Cologne. His articles attracted the attention of the Prussian police, which closed down the newspaper and forced Marx to flee to Paris in 1843. Soon he was expelled from Paris as well, and after some time spent in Brussels, he returned to Paris and then to Germany during the revolutionary upheavals around 1848. In 1849, with the help of Friedrich Engels, he finally immigrated to London, where he remained until the end of his life. Marx's life was thus spent moving among different languages and cultures. Perhaps through the experience of exile, Marx came to recognize the peculiar force of globalization that was transforming the world. However, rather than simply fantasizing about a return to his native land, he imagined a new international world in which national boundaries would become less significant.

Globalization was such a central concern for Marx and Engels that it shaped the very writing of the *Manifesto*. The paragraph celebrating bourgeois globalization cited above culminates in the phrase "world literature": "National one-sidedness and narrow-mindedness become more and more impossible, and from the numerous national and local literatures there arises a world literature." At the time when Marx and Engels wrote the *Manifesto*, the notion that there existed something called "world literature" was relatively new. The term had been coined a few decades earlier by the German writer Johann Wolfgang von Goethe, who wanted to expand the canon of literature to include lesser-known literatures produced either on the periphery of Europe or outside Europe. Goethe recognized that the world was becoming more interdependent not only in material matters but also with respect to literature. Marx and Engels took this notion of "world literature" and adopted it to their own purposes: Their own *Manifesto* was to become world literature too. More than any other text, it was written for a globalized world and more than any other text it addressed itself not to a particular, local, or national readership, but to a worldwide one. Its final, resounding slogan was: "Working men of all countries, unite!" (p. 41).

How can a text become world literature? The key, Marx and Engels recognized, was translation. The preamble of the *Manifesto* announced that "Communists of various nationalities have assembled in London and sketched the following Manifesto, to be published in the English, French, German, Italian, Flemish and Danish languages" (p. 5). Marx and Engels do not even mention that the *Manifesto* was originally written in German, so concerned are they that it be published, simultaneously, in the six languages listed. This demand certainly registers their global aspirations and it also indicates how little they were concerned with the notion of an original language. The only thing that counts is translation, publication, and distribution.[1] In fact, the sentence quoted above mentions as authors not Marx and Engels, but "Communists of various nationalities" who have putatively "sketched" the *Manifesto*. The *Manifesto* presents itself as a text written by many authors, coming from many countries and speaking many languages, a text that therefore seeks to be published in as many countries and languages.

The claim that the *Manifesto* had been written by an international collective of authors and published in six languages registers this text's desire to be world literature, but it does not describe the actual history of its composition and publication. True, the Communist League commissioned Marx and Engels to collaborate on a foundational text, and this function certainly influenced the two authors: They were writing not for themselves, but on behalf of a group, a party. Nevertheless, Marx and Engels alone wrote the actual text. Engels had composed a short first draft in the form of a credo consisting of questions and answers. The final text of the *Manifesto* still bears traces for this earliest draft, especially in part II, which begins with the question "In what relation do the Communists stand to the proletarians as a whole?" (p. 20), which is followed by the correct answer: "The Communists do not form a separate party opposed to other working-class parties." In the process of writing his credo, however, Engels himself began to have doubts about this form. In February 1847, he therefore writes to Marx: "Think a little about the confession of faith. I believe that the best thing is to do away with the catechism form and give the thing the title: Communist *Manifesto*. We have to bring in a certain amount of history, and the present form does not lend itself to this very well. I take with me from Paris what I have written; it is a simple narrative, but miserably composed, in an awful hurry. . . ."[2] In other words, Engels recognized that the question and answer form, reminiscent of a catechism, may be good at distinguishing correct claims about communism from false ones, but not at synthesizing the entire history of capitalism into a compelling narrative. One need only compare the passages rooted in the credo with the energy, the forward drive, the suspenseful account of class struggles presented in other parts of this text to appreciate how fundamental the change from credo to manifesto really was. Engels later credited Marx with having written most of the final text of the *Manifesto*. However, the credit for having recognized the inefficiency of the credo form belongs to Engels.

Just as the claim about collective authorship was exaggerated, so was the project of the *Manifesto*'s simultaneous publication in six languages. The first publication was in German, first as a pamphlet and then in serialized form in a German-language newspaper called *Deutsch-Londoner Zeitung*.[3] Translations into other languages happened only slowly, however, and intermittently. The only other language in which the *Manifesto* appeared in 1848 was Swedish. It took two years for the first English translation to appear; the next complete translation, into Russian, did not appear until 1869, followed by one into Serbian one year later and by the first complete French edition in 1872. For a Danish edition, also promised in the preamble, one had to wait until 1885, for the Italian one until 1890, and the Flemish one until 1892. But if the first decades of the *Manifesto* were less than successful, things changed in the last decade of the nineteenth century, when there was a steep increase in the number of editions and translations. In the early twentieth century, the number of editions increased exponentially, and after the Russian Revolution of 1917, which seemingly validated the *Manifesto*'s predictions and demands, the *Manifesto* was catapulted into world history. Now it also enjoyed increasing distribution outside Europe, where it contributed to the freedom struggles of colonized peoples around the globe. The *Manifesto*'s worldwide success thus occurred only after a significant delay of many decades, but when it finally occurred, it did so with an overwhelming force that no one, including its authors, would have dared to predict. One lesson to be learned from this publication history is that texts should not be dismissed as ineffective just because they fail to leave their mark immediately after their composition. Some texts, such as the *Manifesto*, go underground and work in secret, only to reappear when no one would have expected it. Just as it was premature to declare the *Manifesto* dead after the failure of the Revolutions of 1848, it may be premature to declare it dead after the collapse of communism in 1989.

The history of the *Manifesto* in the nineteenth century is registered in the different prefaces written by Marx and Engels, and, after Marx's death, by Engels alone. In the prefaces, the authors count and list eagerly all attempted and successful editions and translations of their text and report, with increasing pride, its increasing visibility and influence. While willing to admit to certain omissions and mistakes, however, they held onto their basic theses, and given the *Manifesto*'s belated success in the twentieth century, we can say that they were right to leave the text as it was even when history seemed to bypass it during its first few decades.

What were the features that enabled the *Manifesto* to survive its first bleak period and to thrive many decades after its composition? The first was undoubtedly Marx's gift as a writer. The *Manifesto* presents a suspenseful narrative that is structured around imaginary scenes in which different protagonists meet and combat one another. In the opening pages, communism makes a first appearance as a specter in a formulation that surely belongs to one of the most often quoted lines in literature: "A specter is haunting Europe—the specter of Communism" (p. 5). Indeed, Marx often quoted from the history of drama, in particular from Shakespeare, thus enriching his text and interweaving it with the history of literature.[4] After the haunted opening scene, Marx abruptly switches his mode from theater to history, but this history, too, he presents as a high-stakes drama leading up to a single showdown. Marx manages to summarize thousands of years of political and social history by reducing it to a history of class struggle that gets increasingly fierce but also increasingly simple. While earlier societies were organized in hierarchies determined by inherited privileges, industrial societies increasingly do away with class distinctions based on guilds, landed gentry, and feudal overlords. What remains are only two main classes, the laboring poor—the proletariat—who own nothing but their own labor power, which they are forced to sell for increasingly small sums to the second class, the bourgeoisie. This bourgeoisie, for Marx, is the capitalist class as such, the class that is able, through its possession of the means of production, to extract a profit from the labor performed by the proletariat. Nevertheless, for much of the history outlined by Marx, the bourgeoisie is the main protagonist, a veritable hero who manages to beat into submission all the other classes, including the aristocracy, the clergy, and the landowners, all those who cling to their inherited privileges and powers. They are struck down one by one by the bourgeoisie, which turns the world upside down and becomes its true ruler.

Then, however, there is a second shift, an unexpected turn in the plot. In order to accomplish its breathtaking feats, the bourgeoisie has created a helper—namely, the proletariat. At first nothing but a weak lackey, this creature now begins to threaten its creator and can no longer be controlled. It is at this point that the *Manifesto* stops its historical account. We have arrived in the present. The proletariat is still in chains but is flexing its muscles. It has grown strong and already outnumbers the bourgeoisie, which realizes that it must now control a waking giant. Having read about the fate of the aristocracy at the hands of the bourgeoisie, we know what will happen next. The proletariat will break its chains: It will break the brutal rule of the bourgeoisie and deal with its oppressor exactly the way the bourgeoisie had dealt with its own. History thus prefigures the future.

This future, however, will not come about by itself. If the proletariat is going to win this final and all-encompassing battle, it needs to unite. To be sure, the bourgeoisie is divided, namely into different nation states that fight against one another indirectly in the colonies and directly in Europe. But one force unites the bourgeoisie, and that is capitalism. No matter how many battles and wars are fought among bourgeois countries, capitalism will always form a common front against the proletariat on whose exploitation the bourgeois way of life is premised. Capitalism, however, unites not only the bourgeoisie but also the proletariat, which finds itself in the same exploited position everywhere. This unification, however, is merely negative. The whole point of communism and of the *Manifesto* is to turn this negative unity into a positive one, to endow the proletariat with a clear knowledge of the mechanism of its exploitation. To bring about this knowledge, the condition for unification, the *Manifesto* must do more than simply tell the history of different classes and the battles among them. It must convince the proletariat that it forms but one single class, a class furthermore that will fulfill the history of class struggles.

When we read the *Manifesto* today, we should also read it as a compelling and original model of political writing. Marx and Engels effectively invented a new form of political articulation, a mixture of grand history and passionate prose. The *Manifesto* includes practical suggestions, a course of action for communists in the immediate future. But if that were all it did, we would not be reading this text today. It has remained a vital document because it connected particular demands and problems to a larger vision; it risked going beyond the present, reaching back into the distant past in order to create a trajectory into the future. Marx and Engels were thus both shrewd and bold; they created a new form that managed to combine tactical advice and a grand vision for the future.

This new form of writing was used as a model by some of the twentieth century's most influential writers, from Vladimir Lenin and Leon Trotsky to Franz Fanon. Inspired by Marx, political activists and theorists forged new and timely modes of writing. But not only in politics did the *Manifesto* make itself felt. Artists, too, recognized the new and compelling mode of writing that characterized the *Manifesto* and therefore began to import this mode into the sphere of art. Beginning with the late nineteenth century, more and more artistic programs, foundational documents of artistic schools, and texts demanding a new fusion of art and politics were written and labeled "manifesto." The history of twentieth-century art is marked by countless "isms," from futurism and dadaism to surrealism and creationism, and they came into existence through different forms of art manifestos.[5] A broad view of twentieth-century art reveals different periods of manifesto writing, which coincide with periods of revolutionary activity, first in the late 1910s and early 1920s and then again in the late 1960s. Even in recent history, manifestos have shaped the production of art; one example is the "Dogma 95" manifesto (1995), which inspired the production of dozens of films, some major international successes, according to the doctrine set out in its pages. Art manifestos and political manifestos are thus still being written today, even though we are clearly experiencing a moment in history when new forms of political and artistic articulation, new forms of manifestos, need to be invented. For such a reinvention, however, we can return to Marx and Engels's original *Manifesto* in order to experience its original force.

The *Manifesto* also distinguished itself from its competitors through the rigor of Marx's analysis. While earlier socialist literature, which Marx and Engels critique in the third part of their *Manifesto*, were based on fond hopes and utopian ideals, Marx and Engels sought to identify the forces that shaped history in order to calculate the best way to intervene in them. Only real knowledge of historical processes would allow communism to avoid wasting its energy with premature or belated action. The superiority of Marx's method of analysis, however, made itself felt with greatest clarity not in the optimistic *Manifesto*, but in the text devoted to the painful work of analyzing what went wrong with the Revolution of 1848: the *Eighteenth Brumaire*. While we should turn to the *Manifesto* to learn impassioned political rhetoric, we can learn from the *Eighteenth Brumaire* Marx's rigorous, meticulous, and compelling mode of political analysis.

The *Eighteenth Brumaire* is much more difficult to read than the *Manifesto*. While the *Manifesto* is wide-ranging in its scope, presenting history as a battle among a handful of protagonists, the *Eighteenth Brumaire* offers an in-depth analysis of a period spanning less than three years. It presumes a basic knowledge of this period, from France's February Revolution in 1848 to the coup d'état of Louis Bonaparte in 1851. The sheer number of dates and names Marx refers to are confusing, but they gradually become intelligible as Marx connects them to form a comprehensible narrative and integrates them into his explanatory framework. What makes this wealth of detail even more confusing is that Marx uses as a point of comparison the events of the French Revolution (1789–1799) and its aftermath. We thus have to deal with two sets of names, two sets of dates, two sets of events that are constantly being related to one another.

But the extra effort required is worth it. For Marx's decision to use the French Revolution as a foil for the Revolution of 1848 becomes a point of departure for a whole theory of revolution. The *Eighteenth Brumaire* is a study in repetition, beginning with its title, which derives from the calendar instituted by the French Revolution. Marx goes further and claims that all revolutions have turned back, all have derived their models from the past. This may seem to be a surprising claim, since we now think of revolutions in the opposite way, namely as breaks with the past, as attempts to create new conditions and relations. But it is true that the French revolution began as an attempt to meet current abuses of power with a return to a previous moment in history, with a return to a putatively fairer past. The agents of the French Revolution turned not only to their immediate past, but also to the more distant past, in particular to Roman institutions. In Marx's brief account, they become agents who dress up in Roman costumes and utter Roman slogans: "The heroes as well as the parties and the masses of the old French Revolution, performed the task of their time in Roman costume and with Roman phrases" (p. 63). This description of revolutions as returns also echoes the original meaning of revolution, which was not that of a violent break but rather of a continuously revolving motion— for example, of the stars around the sun.

If such repetitive revolutions worked in the past, however, as they did for the French Revolution, they no longer worked in the nineteenth century. Marx faults the Revolution of 1848 for being nothing but an empty repetition. More particularly, 1848 repeated the French Revolution in reverse. While the French Revolution started with modest demands and became increasingly radical until it reached its most extreme phase under Robespierre and his Reign of Terror, the Revolution of 1848 began with a successful overthrow of Louis Philippe. But each faction then dropped its more progressive allies, thus beginning a process of gradual retreat from the initial demands made by the revolutionized masses. At the end of this process, universal suffrage, one of the main demands of the revolution, had been abolished, along with many other freedoms.

Meanwhile, Louis Bonaparte, who had been voted president of the republic, strikes a ridiculous figure throughout. Marx describes the way in which he had to beg parliament for increasingly large sums of money to finance his extravagant lifestyle. But no one seemed to take him seriously politically. He was an unimpressive figure, inarticulate, hapless, and incapable of formulating policies and projects. And yet, by 1851, he somehow managed to usurp all power in a violent coup d'état. Here, the repetition of the French Revolution finds its farcical end: Instead of the great Napoleon Bonaparte, France now had as its head his ridiculous nephew.

Marx provides a fascinating description of this sad and astonishing process through which a genuine revolution is finally derailed altogether. But he does more. He seeks to explain how a figure such as Louis Bonaparte could seize power in Europe's most cultured and politically advanced country. The answer to this question leads into the heart of Marx's analysis. Marx describes the power-brokering among the different factions in the National Assembly, as well as the shifting interplay of other forces such as the National Guard, the army, and Louis Bonaparte. But he also seeks to identify the respective power bases of these factions. He describes, for example, how the two royalist groups, each supporting a different dynasty, share a common interest against the republicans and social-democrats, but how they necessarily fall apart when it comes to reconciling their different plans for the future. The two dynasties simply cannot be fused, the two pretenders cannot become one, and so their common front must fall apart. Similarly, proletarians and bourgeoisie can unite against the monarchy, but they cannot remain united when it comes to property and wage labor, the fundamental issues that divide the two groups. In this way, Marx not only describes the changing allegiances that characterize this tumultuous period; he also explains the different class interests that come to the fore at various crucial moments.

The *Eighteenth Brumaire* reaches its moment of greatest explanatory power when it comes to capturing the peculiar power base of Louis Napoleon himself. Here Marx points to two groups. The first is the so-called *lumpenproletariat*, which literally means "the proletariat in rags" and which captures all kinds of marginal subgroups that belong neither to the laboring masses nor to the bourgeoisie. Here's how Marx describes the *lumpenproletariat*: "Alongside decayed *roués* [debauched people] with dubious means of subsistence and of dubious origin, alongside ruined and adventurous offshoots of the bourgeoisie, were vagabonds, discharged soldiers, discharged jailbirds, escaped galley slaves, swindlers, mountebanks [charlatans], *lazzaroni* [tramps], pickpockets, tricksters, gamblers, *maquereaus* [pimps], brothel keepers, porters, *literati* [writers and intellectuals], organ-grinders, ragpickers, knife grinders, tinkers, beggars—in short, the whole indefinite, disintegrated mass, thrown hither and thither, which the French term *la bohème*" (pp. 115–116). This excessive list shows Marx's contempt for Louis Bonaparte's peculiar support, which the president managed to organize into the so-called Society of December 10. While the aristocracy, the bourgeoisie, and the proletariat fight and thus neutralize one another, Louis Bonaparte finds his support at the margins of society and has the nerve to present himself as a president of the people.

The *lumpenproletariat*, however, is only one pillar of Louis Bonaparte's power. The second and stronger one is the peasantry. In the end, the failure of the revolution came down to a revolt of the country against the city. The French peasants became gradually more impoverished as prices fell. In addition, they had few means of improving their productivity since they were isolated on small plots of land (a result of the land reform instituted after the French Revolution). Isolation marked this group in other respects as well. The peasants lived apart, continually fighting with each other over increasingly small gains with few means for public exchange and communication. This meant that they never managed to see themselves as a distinct class with distinct class interests. Thus, they were more alienated from one another and from their own interests than the proletariat. The only thing that united them was a distrust of all revolutionary activities, which were mostly centered in the cities. Louis Bonaparte relied on this group of reactionary, isolated, and uneducated peasants when he dissolved the National Assembly, arrested the leaders of the opposition, suspended many rights, and ruled as a dictator.

Marx did not despair at such a surprising and depressing change of events. Even though he himself had invested much energy in the revolution, he was able to pull back and analyze the root causes of its demise. In the process, he drew some general conclusions about revolutions. In one of his best-known paragraphs, he describes the difference between bourgeois revolutions, such as the French Revolution, and proletarian revolutions:

> Bourgeois revolutions, like those of the eighteenth century, storm swiftly from success to success; their dramatic effects outdo each other; men and things seem set in sparkling brilliants; ecstasy is the everyday spirit; but they are short-lived; soon they have attained their zenith, and a long crapulent depression lays hold of society before it learns soberly to assimilate the results of its storm-and-stress period. On the other hand, proletarian revolutions, like those of the nineteenth century, criticize themselves constantly, interrupt themselves continually in their own course, come back to the apparently accomplished in order to begin it afresh, deride with unmerciful thoroughness the inadequacies, weaknesses and paltrinesses of their first attempts, seem to throw down their adversary only in order that he may draw new strength from the earth and rise again, more gigantic, before them, recoil ever and anon from the indefinite prodigiousness of their own aims, until a situation has been created which makes all turning back impossible (p. 67).

The strange course of the Revolution of 1848 is thus not a sign of failure, not a sign that France had somehow fallen behind the achievements of the French Revolution. Rather, it is the first signal of an entirely new type of revolution, one that might seem to move incoherently in fits and starts, without direction, but that actually obeys a new historical logic. Marx notices the oddity of the Revolution of 1848, but he thinks ahead and asks us not to model our understanding of the present on the past. This is precisely what had happened in 1848 and precisely the reason why that revolution went wrong. The revolution had not dared to think of itself as a new type of revolution, as a proletarian revolution, and therefore confusedly and half-heartedly tried to hold onto the old patterns and developments. The result was a fake Napoleon, Louis Bonaparte.

The most important conclusion Marx thus drew from the failure of the 1848 revolution was thus a conclusion about what he called the "modern" revolution. We must not continue to restage old bourgeois revolutions like the French Revolution, but we must recognize the form and trajectory of new, proletarian ones. To articulate this modern revolution, he used an odd phrase, the "poetry" of the revolution. He writes: "The social revolution of the nineteenth century cannot draw its poetry from the past, but only from the future. . . . Earlier revolutions required recollections of past world history in order to drug themselves concerning their own content. In order to arrive at its own content, the revolution of the nineteenth century must let the dead bury their dead" (p. 66). "Poetry" of the revolution does not refer to poems about the revolution. Rather it refers to the language in which the revolution is articulated.[6] If we want to stop repeating the mistakes of the past, Marx is saying, we must invent a new poetry, a new way of writing and thinking about the revolution. Marx himself fulfilled this task more than anyone. He invented new ways of writing and thinking about the revolution, imagining future revolutions, demanding new forms of revolution, and of bringing new types of revolutions about. The two texts collected here, the *Manifesto* and the *Eighteenth Brumaire*, are two such texts in which Marx tried to create a new poetry of the revolution, a poetry that is not based on the past but that tries to fashion the future.

The method of analysis and mode of writing that makes Marx worth reading today can be summed up in the last of his eleventh theses on the German materialist philosopher Ludwig Feuerbach: "Philosophers have only interpreted the world; the point is to change it." Rather than giving up on philosophy and theoretical inquiry, however, Marx sought to transform it. He created a form of philosophy and of writing that would intervene in the world, a philosophy whose interpretation of the world would also at the same time be a way of changing it. The *Eighteenth Brumaire* and the *Manifesto* are both texts that combine philosophy and action. In fact, in Marx's "Thesen über Feuerbach" ("Theses on Feuerbach"), short, condensed, and pithy paragraphs and sentences themselves are part of this project of finding new forms of political articulation.

Originally written some years before the *Manifesto* and the *Eighteenth Brumaire*, "Theses on Feuerbach" was not published during Marx's lifetime (Engels published them in 1888 as an appendix to a longer text on Feuerbach). Yet it contains many of Marx's most fundamental positions and assumptions. In it, Marx sketches what it means to adopt the philosophical position of being a materialist. Materialism does not simply mean to reduce the world of ideas to the material world, as Feuerbach had suggested. Marx articulates a new form of materialism that is based on social relations, on the interaction of human beings, and in particular on education. This important point is summed up in the third thesis: "The materialist doctrine—that circumstances and education change and that changed humans are thus the product of changed circumstances and education—forgets that circumstances are changed by humans and that the educator himself must be educated" (p. 179). This thesis shows how far Marx was from a mechanical or reductionist model in which everything is reduced to material circumstances. Circumstances may determine human nature, but humans can change these circumstances. Humans can be changed by a new education, which in turn can only be brought about by educating the educators. Marx thus opens a space for intervention, for change. We need to keep this space in mind when reading his texts, which were forged to educate educators, to change human circumstances by changing humans. This, perhaps, is the Marx we should look for today, the Marx who knows that it is possible to articulate alternative worlds, alternative modes of organizing our world that are different from the ones that are prevalent today. We need the Marx who sought to articulate these alternatives by creating new forms of writing and thinking. To find access to this Marx, we must not return to the dogmas of the various schools of Marxism, nor to the communist systems of the past, but to Marx's actual writings, the words, phrases, expressions, and forms of his stunning, beautiful, and visionary texts.

Martin Puchner is Associate Professor of English and comparative literature at Columbia University and author of *Stage Fright: Modernism, Anti-Theatricality, and Drama,* as well as of *Poetry of the Revolution: Marx, Manifestos, and the Avant-Gardes* (forthcoming). He publishes in such venues as the *London Review of Books, New Literary History,* the *Journal of the History of Ideas,* the *Yale Journal of Criticism, Theatre Research International, Theatre Journal, Modern Drama, TDR,* and *Criticism,* and he has contributed book chapters to several collections of essays. He has written introductions to Lionel Abel's *Tragedy and Metatheater: Essays on Dramatic Form* and to the Barnes & Noble Classics edition of *Six Plays by Henrik Ibsen.* He is coeditor, with Alan Ackerman, of *Against Theatre: Creative Destructions on the Modernist Stage* and, with Ellen Gainor and Stanton Garner, of the forthcoming *Norton Anthology of Drama.* He is also associate editor of *Theatre Survey.* He regularly gives public lectures at theaters in New York and has been interviewed in a variety of venues, including National Public Radio.

Notes

1. For a fuller account of the *Manifesto* as world literature, see Martin Puchner, *Poetry of the Revolution: Marx, Manifestos, and the Avant-Gardes*, Princeton, NJ: Princeton University Press, forthcoming.

2. Letter of November 23–24, 1847; see Karl Marx and Friedrich Engels, *Werke*, vol. 27 (Berlin: Dietz Verlag, 1963), p. 107.

3. For information on the publication history of the *Manifesto*, consult the excellent bibliography by Bert Andréas, *Le Manifeste Communiste de Marx et Engels: Histoire et Bibliographie 1848–1918*, Milano: Feltrinelli, 1963.

4. See Martin Harries, *Scare Quotes from Shakespeare: Marx, Keynes, and the Language of Reenchantment*, Stanford, CA: Stanford University Press, 2000.

5. See Mary Ann Caws, ed., *Manifesto: A Century of Isms*, Lincoln: University of Nebraska Press, 2001.

6. See also Martin Puchner, *Poetry of the Revolution: Marx, Manifestos, and the Avant-Gardes*, Princeton, NJ: Princeton University Press, forthcoming.

THE COMMUNIST MANIFESTO

AND OTHER WRITINGS

MANIFESTO of the COMMUNIST PARTY

KARL MARX
FRIEDRICH ENGELS

translated by Samuel Moore
revised and edited by Friedrich Engels

A SPECTER IS HAUNTING *Europe—the specter of Communism. All the Powers of old Europe have entered into a holy alliance* to exorcise this specter: Pope and Tsar, Metternich and Guizot, French Radicals and German police spies.*

Where is the party in opposition that has not been decried as Communistic by its opponents in power? Where the Opposition that has not hurled back the branding reproach of Communism against the more advanced opposition parties, as well as against its reactionary adversaries?

Two things result from this fact:

I. Communism is already acknowledged by all European Powers to be itself a Power.

II. It is high time that Communists should openly, in the face of the whole world, publish their views, their aims, their tendencies, and meet this nursery tale of the Specter of Communism with a Manifesto of the party itself.

To this end, Communists of various nationalities have assembled in London and sketched the following Manifesto, to be published in the English, French, German, Italian, Flemish and Danish languages.

---

*Agreement made in 1815 between Russia, the Habsburg Empire, and Prussia, and eventually signed by most European monarchs, to adhere to Christian principles; its underlying intent was to preserve the monarchies against growing revolutionary unrest.

I

*Bourgeois and Proletarians**

THE HISTORY OF ALL hitherto existing society[†] is the history of class struggles.

Freeman and slave, patrician and plebeian, lord and serf, guild-master[‡] and journeyman, in a word, oppressor and oppressed, stood in constant opposition to one another, carried on an uninterrupted, now hidden, now open fight, a fight that each time ended either in a revolutionary reconstitution of society at large or in the common ruin of the contending classes.

In the earlier epochs of history we find almost everywhere a complicated arrangement of society into various orders, a manifold gradation of social rank. In ancient Rome we have patricians, knights, plebeians, slaves; in the Middle Ages, feudal lords, vassals, guild-masters, journeymen, apprentices, serfs; in almost all of these classes, again, subordinate gradations.

The modern bourgeois society that has sprouted from the ruins of feudal society has not done away with class antagonisms. It has

---

*By bourgeoisie is meant the class of modern Capitalists, owners of the means of social production and employers of wage labor. By proletariat, the class of modern wage-laborers who, having no means of production of their own, are reduced to selling their labor power in order to live [Engels's note, 1888].

†That is, all written history. In 1847, the pre-history of society, the social organization existing previous to recorded history, was all but unknown. Since then, Haxthausen discovered common ownership of land in Russia, Maurer proved it to be the social foundation from which all Teutonic races started in history, and by and by village communities were found to be, or to have been, the primitive form of society everywhere from India to Ireland. The inner organization of this primitive Communistic society was laid bare, in its typical form, by Morgan's crowning discovery of the true nature of the *gens* and its relation to the tribe. With the dissolution of these primeval communities society begins to be differentiated into separate and finally antagonistic classes. I have attempted to retrace this process of dissolution in: *Der Ursprung der Familie, des Privateigenthums und des Staats*, 2nd edition, Stuttgart, 1886 [Engels's note, 1888].

‡Guild-master, that is, a full member of a guild, a master within, not a head of a guild [Engels's note, 1888].

but established new classes, new conditions of oppression, new forms of struggle in place of the old ones.

Our epoch, the epoch of the bourgeoisie, possesses, however, this distinctive feature: it has simplified the class antagonisms. Society as a whole is splitting up more and more into two great hostile camps, into two great classes directly facing each other: Bourgeoisie and Proletariat.

From the serfs of the Middle Ages sprang the chartered burghers of the earliest towns. From these burgesses the first elements of the bourgeoisie were developed.

The discovery of America, the rounding of the Cape, opened up fresh ground for the rising bourgeoisie. The East Indian and Chinese markets, the colonization of America, trade with the colonies, the increase in the means of exchange and in commodities generally, gave to commerce, to navigation, to industry, an impulse never before known, and thereby, to the revolutionary element in the tottering feudal society, a rapid development.

The feudal system of industry, under which industrial production was monopolized by closed guilds, now no longer sufficed for the growing wants of the new markets. The manufacturing system took its place. The guild-masters were pushed on one side by the manufacturing middle class; division of labor between the different corporate guilds vanished in the face of division of labor in each single workshop.

Meantime the markets kept ever growing, the demand ever rising. Even manufacture no longer sufficed. Thereupon, steam and machinery revolutionized industrial production. The place of manufacture was taken by the giant, Modern Industry, the place of the industrial middle class by industrial millionaires—the leaders of whole industrial armies, the modern bourgeois.

Modern industry has established the world market, for which the discovery of America paved the way. This market has given an immense development to commerce, to navigation, to communication by land. This development has, in its turn, reacted on the extension of industry; and in proportion as industry, commerce, navigation, railways extended, in the same proportion the bourgeoisie developed, increased its capital, and pushed into the background every class handed down from the Middle Ages.

We see, therefore, how the modern bourgeoisie is itself the product of a long course of development, of a series of revolutions in the modes of production and of exchange.

Each step in the development of the bourgeoisie was accompanied by a corresponding political advance of that class. An oppressed class under the sway of the feudal nobility, an armed and self-governing association in the medieval commune;* here independent urban republic (as in Italy and Germany), there taxable "third estate"† of the monarchy (as in France), afterward, in the period of manufacture proper, serving either the semi-feudal or the absolute monarchy as a counterpoise against the nobility, and, in fact, cornerstone of the great monarchies in general, the bourgeoisie has at last, since the establishment of Modern Industry and of the world market, conquered for itself, in the modern representative State, exclusive political sway. The executive of the modern State is but a committee for managing the common affairs of the whole bourgeoisie.

The bourgeoisie, historically, has played a most revolutionary part.

The bourgeoisie, wherever it has got the upper hand, has put an end to all feudal, patriarchal, idyllic relations. It has pitilessly torn asunder the motley feudal ties that bound man to his "natural superiors," and has left remaining no other nexus between man and man than naked self-interest, than callous "cash payment." It has drowned the most heavenly ecstasies of religious fervor, of chivalrous enthusiasm, of philistine sentimentalism, in the icy water of egotistical calculation. It has resolved personal worth into exchange value, and in place of the numberless indefeasible chartered freedoms has set up that single, unconscionable freedom—Free Trade.

---

*"Commune" was the name taken in France by the nascent towns even before they had conquered from their feudal lords and masters local self-government and political rights as the "Third Estate." Generally speaking, for the economic development of the bourgeoisie, England is here taken as the typical country; for its political development, France [Engels's note, 1888].

This was the name given their urban communities by the townsmen of Italy and France, after they had purchased or wrested their initial rights of self-government from their feudal lords [Engels's note, 1890].

†Social class in feudal Europe made up of the bourgeoisie and proletariat. The aristocracy comprised the First Estate, and the clergy the Second.

In one word, for exploitation, veiled by religious and political illusions, it has substituted naked, shameless, direct, brutal exploitation.

The bourgeoisie has stripped of its halo every occupation hitherto honored and looked up to with reverent awe. It has converted the physician, the lawyer, the priest, the poet, the man of science, into its paid wage-laborers.

The bourgeoisie has torn away from the family its sentimental veil, and has reduced the family relation to a mere money relation.

The bourgeoisie has disclosed how it came to pass that the brutal display of vigor in the Middle Ages, which Reactionists so much admire, found its fitting complement in the most slothful indolence. It has been the first to show what man's activity can bring about. It has accomplished wonders far surpassing Egyptian pyramids, Roman aqueducts and Gothic cathedrals; it has conducted expeditions that put in the shade all former Exoduses of nations and crusades.

The bourgeoisie cannot exist without constantly revolutionizing the instruments of production, and thereby the relations of production, and with them the whole relations of society. Conservation of the old modes of production in unaltered form was, on the contrary, the first condition of existence for all earlier industrial classes. Constant revolutionizing of production, uninterrupted disturbance of all social conditions, everlasting uncertainty and agitation distinguish the bourgeois epoch from all earlier ones. All fixed, fast-frozen relations, with their train of ancient and venerable prejudices and opinions, are swept away, all new-formed ones become antiquated before they can ossify. All that is solid melts into air, all that is holy is profaned, and man is at last compelled to face with sober senses his real conditions of life and his relations with his kind.

The need of a constantly expanding market for its products chases the bourgeoisie over the whole surface of the globe. It must nestle everywhere, settle everywhere, establish connections everywhere.

The bourgeoisie has through its exploitation of the world market given a cosmopolitan character to production and consumption in every country. To the great chagrin of Reactionists, it has drawn from under the feet of industry the national ground on which it stood. All old-established national industries have been destroyed or are daily being destroyed. They are dislodged by new industries, whose introduction becomes a life and death question for all civilized nations, by industries that no longer work up indigenous raw material but raw material drawn from the remotest zones; industries whose products are consumed, not only at home, but in every quarter of the globe. In place of the old wants, satisfied by the production of the country, we find new wants, requiring for their satisfaction the products of distant lands and climes. In place of the old local and national seclusion and self-sufficiency, we have intercourse in every direction, universal interdependence of nations. And as in material, so also in intellectual production. The intellectual creations of individual nations become common property. National one-sidedness and narrow-mindedness become more and more impossible, and from the numerous national and local literatures there arises a world literature.*

The bourgeoisie, by the rapid improvement of all instruments of production, by the immensely facilitated means of communication, draws all, even the most barbarian, nations into civilization. The cheap prices of its commodities are the heavy artillery with which it batters down all Chinese walls, with which it forces the barbarians' intensely obstinate hatred of foreigners to capitulate. It compels all nations, on pain of extinction, to adopt the bourgeois mode of production; it compels them to introduce what it calls civilization into their midst, i.e., to become bourgeois themselves. In a word, it creates a world after its own image.

The bourgeoisie has subjected the country to the rule of the towns. It has created enormous cities, has greatly increased the urban population as compared with the rural, and has thus rescued a considerable part of the population from the idiocy of rural life. Just as it has made the country dependent on the towns, so it has made barbarian and semi-barbarian countries dependent on the civilized ones, nations of peasants on nations of bourgeois, the East on the West.

The bourgeoisie keeps doing away more and more with the scat-

---

*Term coined by Johann Wolfgang von Goethe (1749–1832); it reflects his belief that recognizing increasing connections among different European and non-European literatures could be a means for advancing civilization through mutual understanding.

tered state of the population, of the means of production, and of property. It has agglomerated population, centralized means of productions and has concentrated property in a few hands. The necessary consequence of this was political centralization. Independent or but loosely connected provinces with separate interests, laws, governments and systems of taxation became lumped together into one nation, with one government, one code of laws, one national class interest, one frontier and one customs tariff.

The bourgeoisie during its rule of scarce one hundred years has created more massive and more colossal productive forces than have all preceding generations together. Subjection of nature's forces to man, machinery, application of chemistry to industry and agriculture, steam navigation, railways, electric telegraphs, clearing of whole continents for cultivation, canalization of rivers, whole populations conjured out of the ground—what earlier century had even a presentiment that such productive forces slumbered in the lap of social labor?

We see then: the means of production and of exchange, on the foundation of which the bourgeoisie built itself up, were generated in feudal society. At a certain stage in the development of these means of production and of exchange, the conditions under which feudal society produced and exchanged, the feudal organization of agriculture and manufacturing industry, in a word, the feudal relations of property became no longer compatible with the already developed productive forces; they became so many fetters. They had to be burst asunder; they were burst asunder.

Into their place stepped free competition, accompanied by a social and political constitution adapted to it and by the economic and political sway of the bourgeois class.

A similar movement is going on before our own eyes. Modern bourgeois society with its relations of production, of exchange and of property, a society that has conjured up such gigantic means of production and of exchange, is like the sorcerer who is no longer able to control the powers of the nether world whom he has called up by his spells. For many a decade past the history of industry and commerce is but the history of the revolt of modern productive forces against modern conditions of production, against the property relations that are the conditions for the existence of the bourgeoisie and of its rule. It is enough to mention the commercial crises that by their periodical return put on trial, each time more threateningly, the existence of the entire bourgeois society. In these crises a great part not only of the existing products, but also of the previously created productive forces, are periodically destroyed. In these crises there breaks out an epidemic that in all earlier epochs would have seemed an absurdity—the epidemic of over-production. Society suddenly finds itself put back into a state of momentary barbarism; it appears as if a famine, a universal war of devastation had cut off the supply of every means of subsistence; industry and commerce seem to be destroyed; and why? Because there is too much civilization, too much means of subsistence, too much industry, too much commerce. The productive forces at the disposal of society no longer tend to further the development of the conditions of bourgeois property; on the contrary, they have become too powerful for these conditions, by which they are fettered, and as soon as they overcome these fetters, they bring disorder into the whole of bourgeois society, endanger the existence of bourgeois property. The conditions of bourgeois society are too narrow to comprise the wealth created by them. And how does the bourgeoisie get over these crises? On the one hand by enforced destruction of a mass of productive forces; on the other, by the conquest of new markets and by the more thorough exploitation of the old ones. That is to say, by paving the way for more extensive and more destructive crises and by diminishing the means whereby crises are prevented.

The weapons with which the bourgeoisie felled feudalism to the ground are now turned against the bourgeoisie itself.

But not only has the bourgeoisie forged the weapons that bring death to itself; it has also called into existence the men who are to wield those weapons—the modern working class, the proletarians.

In proportion as the bourgeoisie, i.e., capital, is developed, in the same proportion is the proletariat, the modern working class, developed—a class of laborers who live only as long as they find work, and who find work only as long as their labor increases capital. These laborers, who must sell themselves piecemeal, are a commodity like every other article of commerce, and are consequently exposed to all the vicissitudes of competition, to all the fluctuations of the market.

Owing to the extensive use of machinery and to division of labor, the work of the proletarians has lost all individual character and, consequently, all charm for the workman. He becomes an appendage of the machine, and it is only the most simple, most monotonous, and most easily acquired knack that is required of him. Hence, the cost of production of a workman is restricted almost entirely to the means of subsistence that he requires for his maintenance and for the propagation of his race. But the price of a commodity, and therefore also of labor, is equal to its cost of production. In proportion, therefore, as the repulsiveness of the work increases, the wage decreases. Nay more, in proportion as the use of machinery and division of labor increase, in the same proportion the burden of toil also increases, whether by prolongation of the working hours, by increase of the work exacted in a given time or by increased speed of the machinery, etc.

Modern industry has converted the little workshop of the patriarchal master into the great factory of the industrial capitalist. Masses of laborers, crowded into the factory, are organized like soldiers. As privates of the industrial army they are placed under the command of a perfect hierarchy of officers and sergeants. Not only are they slaves of the bourgeois class and of the bourgeois State; they are daily and hourly enslaved by the machine, by the overseer and, above all, by the individual bourgeois manufacturer himself. The more openly this despotism proclaims gain to be its end and aim, the more petty, the more hateful and the more embittering it is.

The less the skill and exertion of strength implied in manual labor, in other words, the more modern industry becomes developed, the more is the labor of men superseded by that of women. Differences of age and sex no longer have any distinctive social validity for the working class. All are instruments of labor, more or less expensive to use, according to their age and sex.

No sooner is the exploitation of the laborer by the manufacturer so far at an end that he receives his wages in cash, than he is set upon by the other portions of the bourgeoisie, the landlord, the shopkeeper, the pawnbroker, etc.

The lower strata of the middle class—the small tradespeople, shopkeepers and retired tradesmen generally, the handicraftsmen and peasants—all these sink gradually into the proletariat, partly because their diminutive capital does not suffice for the scale on which Modern Industry is carried on and is swamped in the competition with the large capitalists, partly because their specialized skill is rendered worthless by new methods of production. Thus the proletariat is recruited from all classes of the population.

The proletariat goes through various stages of development. With its birth begins its struggle with the bourgeoisie. At first the contest is carried on by individual laborers, then by the work people of a factory, then by the operatives of one trade in one locality against the individual bourgeois who directly exploits them. They direct their attacks not against the bourgeois conditions of production, but against the instruments of production themselves; they destroy imported wares that compete with their labor, they smash machinery to pieces, they set factories ablaze, they seek to restore by force the vanished status of the workman of the Middle Ages.

At this stage the laborers still form an incoherent mass scattered over the whole country and broken up by their mutual competition. If anywhere they unite to form more compact bodies, this is not yet the consequence of their own active union but of the union of the bourgeoisie, which class, in order to attain its own political ends, is compelled to set the whole proletariat in motion and, moreover is, for a time, yet able to do so. At this stage, therefore, the proletarians do not fight their enemies, but the enemies of their enemies, the remnants of absolute monarchy, the landowners, the non-industrial bourgeois, the petty bourgeoisie. Thus the whole historical movement is concentrated in the hands of the bourgeoisie; every victory so obtained is a victory for the bourgeoisie.

But with the development of industry the proletariat not only increases in number; it becomes concentrated in greater masses, its strength grows, and it feels that strength more. The various interests and conditions of life within the ranks of the proletariat are more and more equalized in proportion as machinery obliterates all distinctions of labor and nearly everywhere reduces wages to the same low level. The growing competition among the bourgeois, and the resulting commercial crises, make the wages of the workers ever more fluctuating. The unceasing improvement of machinery, ever more rapidly developing, makes their livelihood more and more precarious; the collisions between individual workmen and individ-

ual bourgeois take more and more the character of collisions between two classes. Thereupon the workers begin to form combinations (Trades' Unions) against the bourgeois; they club together in
order to keep up the rate of wages; they found permanent associations in order to make provision beforehand for these occasional revolts. Here and there the contest breaks out into riots.

Now and then the workers are victorious, but only for a time. The
real fruit of their battles lies, not in the immediate result, but in the
ever expanding union of the workers. This union is helped on by
the improved means of communication that are created by modern
industry and that place the workers of different localities in contact
with one another. It was just this contact that was needed to centralize the numerous local struggles, all of the same character, into one
national struggle between classes. But every class struggle is a political struggle. And that union, to attain which the burghers of the
Middle Ages with their miserable highways required centuries, the
modern proletarians, thanks to railways, achieve in a few years.

This organization of the proletarians into a class and consequently into a political party is continually being upset again by the
competition between the workers themselves. But it ever rises up
again, stronger, firmer, mightier. It compels legislative recognition of
particular interests of the workers, by taking advantage of the divisions among the bourgeoisie itself. Thus the ten-hours' bill in England was carried.

Altogether, collisions between the classes of the old society in
many ways further the course of development of the proletariat. The
bourgeoisie finds itself involved in a constant battle. At first with the
aristocracy; later on, with those portions of the bourgeoisie itself
whose interests have become antagonistic to the progress of industry; at all times with the bourgeoisie of foreign countries. In all these
battles it sees itself compelled to appeal to the proletariat, to ask for
its help, and thus to drag it into the political arena. The bourgeoisie
itself, therefore, supplies the proletariat with its own elements of political and general education; in other words, it furnishes the proletariat with weapons for fighting the bourgeoisie.

Further, as we have already seen, entire sections of the ruling
classes are precipitated into the proletariat by the advance of industry, or are at least threatened in their conditions of existence. These

also supply the proletariat with fresh elements of enlightenment and progress.

Finally, in times when the class struggle nears the decisive hour, the process of dissolution going on within the ruling class, in fact within the whole range of old society, assumes such a violent, glaring character that a small section of the ruling class cuts itself adrift and joins the revolutionary class, the class that holds the future in its hands. Therefore, just as, at an earlier period a section of the nobility went over to the bourgeoisie, so now a portion of the bourgeoisie goes over to the proletariat, and in particular a portion of the bourgeois ideologists who have raised themselves to the level of comprehending theoretically the historical movement as a whole.

Of all the classes that stand face to face with the bourgeoisie today, the proletariat alone is a really revolutionary class. The other classes decay and finally disappear in the face of modern industry; the proletariat is its special and essential product.

The lower middle class, the small manufacturer, the shopkeeper, the artisan, the peasant, all these fight against the bourgeoisie to save from extinction their existence as fractions of the middle class. They are therefore not revolutionary, but conservative. Nay more, they are reactionary, for they try to roll back the wheel of history. If by chance they are revolutionary, they are so only in view of their impending transfer into the proletariat; they thus defend not their present, but their future interests; they desert their own standpoint to place themselves at that of the proletariat.

The "dangerous class," the social scum, that passively rotting mass thrown off by the lowest layers of the old society may here and there be swept into the movement by a proletarian revolution; its conditions of life, however, prepare it far more for the part of a bribed tool of reactionary intrigue.

In the conditions of the proletariat, those of the old society at large are already virtually swamped. The proletarian is without property; his relation to his wife and children has no longer anything in common with the bourgeois family relations; modern industrial labor, modern subjection to capital, the same in England as in France, in America as in Germany, has stripped him of every trace of national character. Law, morality, religion are to him so many bourgeois prejudices behind which lurk in ambush just as many bourgeois interests.

All the preceding classes that got the upper hand sought to fortify their already acquired status by subjecting society at large to their conditions of appropriation. The proletarians cannot become masters of the productive forces of society except by abolishing their own previous mode of appropriation, and thereby also every other previous mode of appropriation. They have nothing of their own to secure and to fortify; their mission is to destroy all previous securities for, and insurances of, individual property.

All previous historical movements were movements of minorities or in the interest of minorities. The proletarian movement is the self-conscious, independent movement of the immense majority in the interest of the immense majority. The proletariat, the lowest stratum of our present society, cannot stir, cannot raise itself up, without the whole superincumbent strata of official society being sprung into the air.

Though not in substance, yet in form, the struggle of the proletariat with the bourgeoisie is at first a national struggle. The proletariat of each country must, of course, first of all settle matters with its own bourgeoisie.

In depicting the most general phases of the development of the proletariat, we traced the more or less veiled civil war raging within existing society up to the point where that war breaks out into open revolution, and where the violent overthrow of the bourgeoisie lays the foundation for the sway of the proletariat.

Hitherto, every form of society has been based, as we have already seen, on the antagonism of oppressing and oppressed classes. But in order to oppress a class certain conditions must be assured to it under which it can, at least, continue its slavish existence. The serf, in the period of serfdom, raised himself to membership in the commune, just as the petty bourgeois, under the yoke of feudal absolutism, managed to develop into a bourgeois. The modern laborer, on the contrary, instead of rising with the progress of industry sinks deeper and deeper below the conditions of existence of his own class. He becomes a pauper, and pauperism develops more rapidly than population and wealth. And here it becomes evident that the bourgeoisie is unfit any longer to be the ruling class in society and to impose its conditions of existence upon society as an over-riding law. It is unfit to rule because it is incompetent to assure an existence to its slave within his slavery, because it cannot help letting him sink into such a state that it has to feed him instead of being fed by him. Society can no longer live under this bourgeoisie, in other words, its existence is no longer compatible with society.

The essential condition for the existence and for the sway of the bourgeois class is the formation and augmentation of capital; the condition for capital is wage labor. Wage labor rests exclusively on competition between the laborers. The advance of industry, whose involuntary promoter is the bourgeoisie, replaces the isolation of the laborers, due to competition, by their revolutionary combination due to association. The development of Modern Industry therefore cuts from under its feet the very foundation on which the bourgeoisie produces and appropriates products. What the bourgeoisie therefore produces, above all, are its own grave-diggers. Its fall and the victory of the proletariat are equally inevitable.

II

Proletarians and Communists

IN WHAT RELATION DO the Communists stand to the proletarians as a whole?

The Communists do not form a separate party opposed to other working-class parties.

They have no interests separate and apart from those of the proletariat as a whole.

They do not set up any sectarian principles of their own by which to shape and mold the proletarian movement.

The Communists are distinguished from the other working-class parties by this only: (1) In the national struggles of the proletarians of the different countries they point out and bring to the front the common interests of the entire proletariat, independently of all nationality. (2) In the various stages of development which the struggle of the working class against the bourgeoisie has to pass through, they always and everywhere represent the interests of the movement as a whole.

The Communists therefore are on the one hand, practically, the most advanced and resolute section of the working-class parties of every country, that section which pushes forward all others; on the other hand, theoretically, they have over the great mass of the proletariat the advantage of clearly understanding the line of march, the conditions, and the ultimate general results of the proletarian movement.

The immediate aim of the Communists is the same as that of all the other proletarian parties: formation of the proletariat into a class, overthrow of the bourgeois supremacy, conquest of political power by the proletariat.

The theoretical conclusions of the Communists are in no way based on ideas or principles that have been invented or discovered by this or that would-be universal reformer.

They merely express, in general terms, actual relations springing from an existing class struggle, from a historical movement going on under our very eyes. The abolition of existing property relations is not at all a distinctive feature of Communism.

All property relations in the past have continually been subject to historical change consequent upon the change in historical conditions.

The French Revolution, for example, abolished feudal property in favor of bourgeois property.

The distinguishing feature of Communism is not the abolition of property generally, but the abolition of bourgeois property. But modern bourgeois private property is the final and most complete expression of the system of producing and appropriating products, that is based on class antagonisms, on the exploitation of the many by the few.

In this sense, the theory of the Communists may be summed up in the single sentence: Abolition of private property.

We Communists have been reproached with the desire of abolishing the right of personally acquiring property as the fruit of a man's own labor, which property is alleged to be the groundwork of all personal freedom, activity and independence.

Hard-won, self-acquired, self-earned property! Do you mean the property of the petty artisan and of the small peasant, a form of property that preceded the bourgeois form? There is no need to abolish that; the development of industry has to a great extent already destroyed it, and is still destroying it daily.

Or do you mean modern bourgeois private property?

But does wage labor create any property for the laborer? Not a bit. It creates capital, i.e., that kind of property which exploits wage labor and which cannot increase except upon condition of begetting a new supply of wage labor for fresh exploitation. Property, in its present form, is based on the antagonism of capital and wage labor. Let us examine both sides of this antagonism.

To be a capitalist, is to have not only a purely personal but a social *status* in production. Capital is a collective product, and only by the united action of many members, nay, in the last resort, only by the united action of all members of society, can it be set in motion.

Capital is, therefore, not a personal, it is a social power.

When therefore capital is converted into common property, into the property of all members of society, personal property is not thereby transformed into social property. It is only the social character of the property that is changed. It loses its class character.

Let us now take wage labor.

The average price of wage labor is the minimum wage, i.e., that quantum of the means of subsistence which is absolutely requisite to keep the laborer in bare existence as a laborer. What, therefore, the wage-laborer appropriates by means of his labor merely suffices to prolong and reproduce a bare existence. We by no means intend to abolish this personal appropriation of the products of labor, an appropriation that is made for the maintenance and reproduction of human life and that leaves no surplus wherewith to command the labor of others. All that we want to do away with is the miserable character of this appropriation, under which the laborer lives merely to increase capital and is allowed to live only in so far as the interest of the ruling class requires it.

In bourgeois society, living labor is but a means to increase accumulated labor. In Communist society, accumulated labor is but a means to widen, to enrich, to promote the existence of the laborer.

In bourgeois society, therefore, the past dominates the present; in Communist society the present dominates the past. In bourgeois society capital is independent and has individuality, while the living person is dependent and has no individuality.

And the abolition of this state of things is called by the bourgeois abolition of individuality and freedom! And rightly so. The abolition of bourgeois individuality, bourgeois independence and bourgeois freedom is undoubtedly aimed at.

By freedom is meant, under the present bourgeois conditions of production, free trade, free selling and buying.

But if selling and buying disappears, free selling and buying disappears also. This talk about free selling and buying and all the other "brave words" of our bourgeoisie about freedom in general have a meaning, if any, only in contrast with restricted selling and buying, with the fettered traders of the Middle Ages, but have no meaning when opposed to the Communist abolition of buying and selling, of the bourgeois conditions of production, and of the bourgeoisie itself.

You are horrified at our intending to do away with private property. But in your existing society private property is already done away with for nine-tenths of the population; its existence for the few is solely due to its non-existence in the hands of those nine-tenths. You reproach us, therefore, with intending to do away with a form of property, the necessary condition for whose existence is the non-existence of any property for the immense majority of society.

In a word, you reproach us with intending to do away with your property. Precisely so; that is just what we intend.

From the moment when labor can no longer be converted into capital, money, or rent, into a social power capable of being monopolized, i.e., from the moment when individual property can no longer be transformed into bourgeois property, into capital, from that moment, you say, individuality vanishes.

You must, therefore, confess that by "individual" you mean no other person than the bourgeois, than the middle-class owner of property. This person must, indeed, be swept out of the way and made impossible.

Communism deprives no man of the power to appropriate the products of society; all that it does is to deprive him of the power to subjugate the labor of others by means of such appropriation.

It has been objected that upon the abolition of private property all work will cease and universal laziness will overtake us.

According to this, bourgeois society ought long ago to have gone to the dogs through sheer idleness; for those of its members who work acquire nothing, and those who acquire anything do not work. The whole of this objection is but another expression of the tautology: there can no longer be any wage labor when there is no longer any capital.

All objections urged against the Communistic mode of producing and appropriating material products have in the same way been urged against the Communistic modes of producing and appropriating intellectual products. Just as, to the bourgeois, the disappearance of class property is the disappearance of production itself, so the disappearance of class culture is to him identical with the disappearance of all culture.

That culture, the loss of which he laments, is for the enormous majority a mere training to act as a machine.

But don't wrangle with us so long as you apply to our intended abolition of bourgeois property the standard of your bourgeois notions of freedom, culture, law, etc. Your very ideas are but the outgrowth of the conditions of your bourgeois production and bourgeois property, just as your jurisprudence is but the will of your class made into a law for all, a will whose essential character and direction are determined by the economic conditions of existence of your class.

The selfish misconception that induces you to transform into eternal laws of nature and of reason the social forms springing from your present mode of production and form of property—historical relations that rise and disappear in the progress of production—this misconception you share with every ruling class that has preceded you. What you see clearly in the case of ancient property, what you admit in the case of feudal property, you are of course forbidden to admit in the case of your own bourgeois form of property.

Abolition of the family! Even the most radical flare up at this infamous proposal of the Communists.

On what foundation is the present family, the bourgeois family, based? On capital, on private gain. In its completely developed form this family exists only among the bourgeoisie. But this state of things finds its complement in the practical absence of the family among the proletarians, and in public prostitution.

The bourgeois family will vanish as a matter of course when its complement vanishes, and both will vanish with the vanishing of capital.

Do you charge us with wanting to stop the exploitation of children by their parents? To this crime we plead guilty.

But, you will say, we destroy the most hallowed of relations when we replace home education by social.

And your education! Is not that also social, and determined by the social conditions under which you educate, by the intervention, direct or indirect, of society, by means of schools, etc.? The Communists have not invented the intervention of society in education; they do but seek to alter the character of that intervention, and to rescue education from the influence of the ruling class.

The bourgeois claptrap about the family and education, about the hallowed correlation of parent and child, becomes all the more disgusting the more, by the action of Modern Industry, all family ties among the proletarians are torn asunder and their children transformed into simple articles of commerce and instruments of labor.

But you Communists would introduce community of women, screams the whole bourgeoisie in chorus.

The bourgeois sees in his wife a mere instrument of production. He hears that the instruments of production are to be exploited in common, and, naturally, can come to no other conclusion than that the lot of being common to all will likewise fall to the women.

He has not even a suspicion that the real point aimed at is to do away with the status of women as mere instruments of production.

For the rest, nothing is more ridiculous than the virtuous indignation of our bourgeois at the community of women which, they pretend, is to be openly and officially established by the Communists. The Communists have no need to introduce community of women; it has existed almost from time immemorial.

Our bourgeois, not content with having the wives and daughters of their proletarians at their disposal, not to speak of common prostitutes, take the greatest pleasure in seducing each other's wives.

Bourgeois marriage is in reality a system of wives in common and thus, at the most, what the Communists might possibly be reproached with is that they desire to introduce, in substitution for a hypocritically concealed, an openly legalized community of women. For the rest, it is self-evident that the abolition of the present system of production must bring with it the abolition of the community of women springing from that system, i.e., of prostitution both public and private.

The Communists are further reproached with desiring to abolish countries and nationality.

The workingmen have no country. We cannot take from them what they have not got. Since the proletariat must first of all acquire political supremacy, must rise to be the leading class of the nation, must constitute itself as the nation, it is so far itself national, though not in the bourgeois sense of the word.

National differences and antagonisms between peoples are vanishing daily more and more owing to the development of the bourgeoisie, to freedom of commerce, to the world market, to uniformity in the mode of production and in the conditions of life corresponding thereto.

The supremacy of the proletariat will cause them to vanish still faster. United action, of the leading civilized countries at least, is one of the first conditions for the emancipation of the proletariat.

In proportion as the exploitation of one individual by another is put to an end, the exploitation of one nation by another will also be put to an end. In proportion as the antagonism between classes within the nation vanishes, the hostility of one nation to another will come to an end.

The charges against Communism made from a religious, a philosophical and generally from an ideological standpoint, are not deserving of serious examination.

Does it require deep intuition to comprehend that man's ideas, views and conceptions, in one word, man's consciousness, changes with every change in the conditions of his material existence, in his social relations and in his social life?

What else does the history of ideas prove than that intellectual production changes its character in proportion as material production is changed? The ruling ideas of each age have ever been the ideas of its ruling class.

When people speak of ideas that revolutionize society they do but express the fact that within the old society the elements of a new one have been created, and that the dissolution of the old ideas keeps even pace with the dissolution of the old conditions of existence.

When the ancient world was in its last throes the ancient religions were overcome by Christianity. When Christian ideas succumbed in the 18th century to rationalist ideas, feudal society fought its death battle with the then revolutionary bourgeoisie. The ideas of religious liberty and freedom of conscience merely gave expression to the sway of free competition within the domain of knowledge.

"Undoubtedly," it will be said, "religious, moral, philosophical and juridical ideas have been modified in the course of historical development. But religion, morality, philosophy, political science, and law, constantly survived this change.

"There are, besides, eternal truths, such as Freedom, Justice, etc., that are common to all states of society. But Communism abolishes eternal truths, it abolishes all religion and all morality, instead of constituting them on a new basis; it therefore acts in contradiction to all past historical experience."

What does this accusation reduce itself to? The history of all past society has consisted in the development of class antagonisms, antagonisms that assumed different forms at different epochs.

But whatever form they may have taken, one fact is common to all past ages, viz., the exploitation of one part of society by the other. No wonder, then, that the social consciousness of past ages, despite all the multiplicity and variety it displays, moves within certain common forms, or general ideas, which cannot completely vanish except with the total disappearance of class antagonisms.

The Communist revolution is the most radical rupture with traditional property relations; no wonder that its development involves the most radical rupture with traditional ideas.

But let us have done with the bourgeois objections to Communism.

We have seen above that the first step in the revolution by the working class is to raise the proletariat to the position of ruling class, to win the battle of democracy.

The proletariat will use its political supremacy to wrest, by degrees, all capital from the bourgeoisie, to centralize all instruments of production in the hands of the State, i.e., of the proletariat organized as the ruling class; and to increase the total of productive forces as rapidly as possible.

Of course, in the beginning this cannot be effected except by means of despotic inroads on the rights of property and on the conditions of bourgeois production; by means of measures, therefore, which appear economically insufficient and untenable but which, in the course of the movement, outstrip themselves, necessitate further inroads upon the old social order, and are unavoidable as a means of entirely revolutionizing the mode of production.

These measures will of course be different in different countries.

Nevertheless in the most advanced countries, the following will be pretty generally applicable:

1. Abolition of property in land and application of all rents of land to public purposes.

2. A heavy progressive or graduated income tax.

3. Abolition of all right of inheritance.

4. Confiscation of the property of all emigrants and rebels.

5. Centralization of credit in the hands of the State, by means of a national bank with State capital and an exclusive monopoly.

6. Centralization of the means of communication and transport in the hands of the State.

7. Extension of factories and instruments of production owned by the State; the bringing into cultivation of wastelands, and the improvement of the soil generally in accordance with a common plan.

8. Equal liability of all to labor. Establishment of industrial armies, especially for agriculture.

9. Combination of agriculture with manufacturing industries; gradual abolition of the distinction between town and country by a more equable distribution of the population over the country.

10. Free education for all children in public schools. Abolition of children's factory labor in its present form. Combination of education with industrial production, etc., etc.

When in the course of development class distinctions have disappeared and all production has been concentrated in the hands of a vast association of the whole nation, the public power will lose its political character. Political power, properly so called, is merely the organized power of one class for oppressing another. If the proletariat during its contest with the bourgeoisie is compelled, by the force of circumstances, to organize itself as a class, if by means of a revolution it makes itself the ruling class and, as such, sweeps away by force the old conditions of production, then it will, along with these conditions, have swept away the conditions for the existence of class antagonisms and of classes generally, and will thereby have abolished its own supremacy as a class.

In place of the old bourgeois society, with its classes and class antagonisms, we shall have an association in which the free development of each is the condition for the free development of all.

III

Socialist and Communist Literature

1. REACTIONARY SOCIALISM

a. Feudal Socialism

OWING TO THEIR HISTORICAL position, it became the vocation of the aristocracies of France and England to write pamphlets against modern bourgeois society. In the French revolution of July 1830 and in English reform agitation these aristocracies again succumbed to the hateful upstart. Thenceforth, a serious political contest was altogether out of question. A literary battle alone remained possible. But even in the domain of literature the old cries of the restoration period* had become impossible.

In order to arouse sympathy, apparently the aristocracy were obliged to lose sight of their own interests, and to formulate their indictment against the bourgeoisie in the interest of the exploited working class alone. Thus the aristocracy took their revenge by singing lampoons on their new master and whispering in his ears sinister prophecies of coming catastrophe.

In this way arose Feudal Socialism: half lamentation, half lampoon; half echo of the past, half menace of the future; at times, by its bitter, witty and incisive criticism, striking the bourgeoisie to the very heart's core; but always ludicrous in its effect through total incapacity to comprehend the march of modern history.

The aristocracy, in order to rally the people to them, waved the proletarian alms-bag in front for a banner. But the people, so often as it joined them, saw on their hindquarters the old feudal coats of arms and deserted with loud and irreverent laughter.

---

*Not the English Restoration, 1660 to 1689, but the French Restoration, 1814 to 1830 [Engels's note, 1888].

One section of the French Legitimists* and "Young England"† exhibited this spectacle.

In pointing out that their mode of exploitation was different than that of the bourgeoisie, the feudalists forget that they exploited under circumstances and conditions that were quite different and that are now antiquated. In showing that under their rule the modern proletariat never existed, they forget that the modern bourgeoisie is the necessary offspring of their own form of society.

For the rest, so little do they conceal the reactionary character of their criticism that their chief accusation against the bourgeoisie amounts to this, that under the bourgeois *régime* a class is being developed which is destined to cut up root and branch the old order of society.

What they upbraid the bourgeoisie with is not so much that it creates a proletariat as that it creates a *revolutionary* proletariat.

In political practice, therefore, they join in all coercive measures against the working class; and in ordinary life, despite their high-falutin phrases, they stoop to pick up the golden apples dropped from the tree of industry and to barter truth, love, and honor for traffic in wool, beetroot-sugar and potato spirits.‡

As the parson has ever gone hand in hand with the landlord, so has Clerical Socialism with Feudal Socialism.

Nothing is easier than to give Christian asceticism a Socialist tinge. Has not Christianity declaimed against private property, against marriage, against the State? Has it not preached in the place of these, charity and poverty, celibacy and mortification of the flesh, monastic life and Mother Church? Christian Socialism is but the holy water with which the priest consecrates the heart-burnings of the aristocrat.

---

*Royalists in France who demanded the return of the older branch of the Bourbon dynasty, which had been overthrown with King Charles X (1757–1836) in the Revolution of 1830.

†Section of the Tory Party that advocated a return to a pre-capitalist society.

‡This applies chiefly to Germany where the landed aristocracy and squirearchy have large portions of their estates cultivated for their own account by stewards, and are, moreover, extensively beetroot-sugar manufacturers and distillers of potato spirits. The wealthier British aristocracy are, as yet, rather above that; but they, too, know how to make up for declining rents by lending their names to floaters of more or less shady joint-stock companies [Engels's note, 1888].

b. Petty-Bourgeois Socialism

The feudal aristocracy was not the only class that was ruined by the bourgeoisie, not the only class whose conditions of existence pined and perished in the atmosphere of modern bourgeois society. The medieval burgesses and the small peasant proprietors were the precursors of the modern bourgeoisie. In those countries which are but little developed, industrially and commercially, these two classes still vegetate side by side with the rising bourgeoisie.

In countries where modern civilization has become fully developed a new class of petty bourgeois has been formed, fluctuating between proletariat and bourgeoisie and ever renewing itself as a supplementary part of bourgeois society. The individual members of this class, however, are being constantly hurled down into the proletariat by the action of competition, and as modern industry develops they even see the moment approaching when they will disappear completely as an independent section of modern society, to be replaced in manufactures, agriculture and commerce by overseers, bailiffs and shopmen.

In countries like France, where the peasants constitute far more than half of the population, it was natural that writers who sided with the proletariat against the bourgeoisie, should use in their criticism of the bourgeois *régime* the standard of the peasant and petty bourgeois, and from the standpoint of these intermediate classes should take up the cudgels for the working class. Thus arose pettybourgeois Socialism. Sismondi* was the head of this school, not only in France but also in England.

This school of Socialism dissected with great acuteness the contradictions in the conditions of modern production. It laid bare the hypocritical apologies of economists. It proved, incontrovertibly, the disastrous effects of machinery and division of labor, the concentration of capital and land in a few hands, over-production and crises; it pointed out the inevitable ruin of the petty bourgeois and peasant, the misery of the proletariat, the anarchy in production, the crying inequalities in the distribution of wealth, the industrial war of ex-

---

*Jean-Charles-Léonard Simonde de Sismondi (1773–1842), Swiss economist who became critical of industrialization and capitalism because of its effects on the poor.

termination between nations, the dissolution of old moral bonds, of the old family relations, of the old nationalities.

In its positive aims, however, this form of Socialism aspires either to restoring the old means of production and of exchange, and with them the old property relations and the old society, or to cramping the modern means of production and of exchange within the framework of the old property relations that have been, and were bound to be, exploded by those means. In either case, it is both reactionary and Utopian.

Its last words are: corporate guilds for manufacture; patriarchal relations in agriculture.

Ultimately, when stubborn historical facts had dispersed all intoxicating effects of self-deception, this form of Socialism ended in a miserable fit of the blues.

c. German or "True" Socialism

The Socialist and Communist literature of France, a literature that originated under the pressure of a bourgeoisie in power and that was the expression of the struggle against this power, was introduced into Germany at a time when the bourgeoisie in that country had just begun its contest with feudal absolutism.

German philosophers, would-be philosophers, and *beaux esprits** eagerly seized on this literature, only forgetting that when these writings immigrated from France into Germany, French social conditions had not immigrated along with them. In contact with German social conditions, this French literature lost all its immediate practical significance and assumed a purely literary aspect. Thus, to the German philosophers of the 18th century, the demands of the first French Revolution were nothing more than the demands of "Practical Reason"† in general, and the utterance of the will of the revolutionary French bourgeoisie signified in their eyes the laws of pure Will, of Will as it was bound to be, of true human Will generally.

---

*Literally, beautiful spirits (French); intelligent and cultivated persons.
†Reference to *The Critique of Practical Reason*, by Immanuel Kant (1724–1804), which was concerned with questions of ethics and politics, as opposed to his *The Critique of Pure Reason*, which dealt with questions of truth.

The work of the German *literati** consisted solely in bringing the new French ideas into harmony with their ancient philosophical conscience or, rather, in annexing the French ideas without deserting their own philosophic point of view.

This annexation took place in the same way in which a foreign language is appropriated, namely, by translation.

It is well known how the monks wrote silly lives of Catholic Saints *over* the manuscripts on which the classical works of ancient heathendom had been written. The German *literati* reversed this process with the profane French literature. They wrote their philosophical nonsense beneath the French original. For instance, beneath the French criticism of the economic functions of money, they wrote "Alienation of Humanity," and beneath the French criticism of the bourgeois State they wrote, "Dethronement of the Category of the General," and so forth.

The introduction of these philosophical phrases at the back of the French historical criticisms they dubbed "Philosophy of Action," "True Socialism," "German Science of Socialism," "Philosophical Foundation of Socialism," and so on.

The French Socialist and Communist literature was thus completely emasculated. And since it ceased in the hands of the German to express the struggle of one class with the other, he felt conscious of having overcome "French one-sidedness" and of representing, not true requirements, but the requirements of Truth; not the interests of the proletariat, but the interests of Human Nature, of Man in general, who belongs to no class, has no reality, who exists only in the misty realm of philosophical fantasy.

This German Socialism, which took its schoolboy task so seriously and solemnly and extolled its poor stock-in-trade in such mountebank fashion, meanwhile gradually lost its pedantic innocence.

The fight of the German and especially of the Prussian bourgeoisie against feudal aristocracy and absolute monarchy, in other words, the liberal movement, became more earnest.

By this, the long-wished-for opportunity was offered to "True" Socialism of confronting the political movement with the Socialist demands, of hurling the traditional anathemas against liberalism,

---

*Writers and intellectuals.

against representative government, against bourgeois competition, bourgeois freedom of the press, bourgeois legislation, bourgeois liberty and equality, and of preaching to the masses that they had nothing to gain, and everything to lose, by this bourgeois movement. German Socialism forgot in the nick of time that the French criticism, whose silly echo it was, presupposed the existence of modern bourgeois society, with its corresponding economic conditions of existence and the political constitution adapted thereto, the very things whose attainment was the object of the pending struggle in Germany.

To the absolute governments, with their following of parsons, professors, country squires and officials, it served as a welcome scarecrow against the threatening bourgeoisie.

It was a sweet finish after the bitter pills of floggings and bullets with which these same governments, just at that time, dosed the German working-class risings.

While this "True" Socialism thus served the governments as a weapon for fighting the German bourgeoisie, at the same time it directly represented a reactionary interest, the interest of the German Philistines. In Germany the *petty-bourgeois* class, a relic of the 16th century, and since then constantly cropping up again under various forms, is the real social basis of the existing state of things.

To preserve this class is to preserve the existing state of things in Germany. The industrial and political supremacy of the bourgeoisie threatens it with certain destruction—on the one hand, from the concentration of capital; on the other, from the rise of a revolutionary proletariat. "True" Socialism appeared to kill these two birds with one stone. It spread like an epidemic.

The robe of speculative cobwebs, embroidered with flowers of rhetoric, steeped in the dew of sickly sentiment, this transcendental robe in which the German Socialists wrapped their sorry "eternal truths," all skin and bone, served wonderfully to increase the sale of their goods amongst such a public.

And on its part, German Socialism recognized more and more its own calling as the bombastic representative of the petty-bourgeois Philistine.

It proclaimed the German nation to be the model nation and the German petty Philistine to be the typical man. To every villainous meanness of this model man it gave a hidden, higher, Socialistic interpretation, the exact contrary of its real character. It went to the extreme length of directly opposing the "brutally destructive" tendency of Communism, and of proclaiming its supreme and impartial contempt of all class struggles. With very few exceptions, all the so-called Socialist and Communist publications that now (1847) circulate in Germany belong to the domain of this foul and enervating literature.*

2. CONSERVATIVE OR BOURGEOIS SOCIALISM

A PART OF THE bourgeoisie is desirous of redressing social grievances in order to secure the continued existence of bourgeois society.

To this section belong economists, philanthropists, humanitarians, improvers of the condition of the working class, organizers of charity, members of societies for the prevention of cruelty to animals, temperance fanatics, hole-and-corner reformers of every imaginable kind. This form of Socialism has, moreover, been worked out into complete systems.

We may cite Proudhon's *Philosophie de la Misère*† as an example of this form.

The Socialistic bourgeois want all the advantages of modern social conditions without the struggles and dangers necessarily resulting therefrom. They desire the existing state of society minus its revolutionary and disintegrating elements. They wish for a bourgeoisie without a proletariat. The bourgeoisie naturally conceives the world in which it is supreme to be the best; and bourgeois Socialism develops this comfortable conception into various more or less complete systems. In requiring the proletariat to carry out such a system, and thereby to march straightway into the social New Jerusalem, it but requires in reality that the proletariat should re-

---

*The revolutionary storm of 1848 swept away this whole shabby tendency and cured its protagonists of the desire to dabble further in Socialism. The chief representative and classical type of this tendency is Herr Karl Grün [Engels's note, 1890].

†Pierre-Joseph Proudhon (1809–1865), French socialist who coined the slogan "property is theft" and published a book entitled *The Philosophy of Poverty*. Marx attacked Proudhon's ideas in a pamphlet called *The Poverty of Philosophy*.

main within the bounds of existing society, but should cast away all its hateful ideas concerning the bourgeoisie.

A second and more practical, but less systematic, form of this Socialism sought to depreciate every revolutionary movement in the eyes of the working class by showing that no mere political reform, but only a change in the material conditions of existence, in economic relations, could be of any advantage to them. By changes in the material conditions of existence this form of Socialism, however, by no means understands abolition of the bourgeois relations of production, an abolition that can be effected only by a revolution, but administrative reforms, based on the continued existence of these relations; reforms, therefore, that in no respect affect the relations between capital and labor, but at the best lessen the cost and simplify the administrative work of bourgeois government.

Bourgeois Socialism attains adequate expression when, and only when, it becomes a mere figure of speech.

Free trade: for the benefit of the working class. Protective duties: for the benefit of the working class. Prison reform: for the benefit of the working class. This is the last word and the only seriously meant word of bourgeois Socialism.

It is summed up in the phrase: the bourgeois is a bourgeois—for the benefit of the working class.

3. CRITICAL-UTOPIAN SOCIALISM AND COMMUNISM

WE DO NOT HERE refer to that literature which in every great modern revolution has always given voice to the demands of the proletariat, such as the writings of Babeuf* and others.

The first direct attempts of the proletariat to attain its own ends—made in times of universal excitement, when feudal society was being overthrown—necessarily failed, owing to the then undeveloped state of the proletariat as well as to the absence of the economic conditions for its emancipation, conditions that had yet to be produced and could be produced by the impending bourgeois epoch alone. The

---

*François-Noël Babeuf (1760–1797) supported the French Revolution and advocated increasingly radical reforms; he formed a secret society, the Conspiracy of the Equals, to overthrow the government and was finally executed.

revolutionary literature that accompanied these first movements of the proletariat had necessarily a reactionary character. It inculcated universal asceticism and social leveling in its crudest form.

The Socialist and Communist systems properly so called, those of St. Simon,* Fourier,† Owen‡ and others, spring into existence in the early undeveloped period, described above, of the struggle between proletariat and bourgeoisie (see Section I. Bourgeois and Proletarians).

The founders of these systems indeed see the class antagonisms as well as the action of the decomposing elements in the prevailing form of society. But the proletariat, as yet in its infancy, offers to them the spectacle of a class without any historical initiative or any independent political movement.

Since the development of class antagonism keeps even pace with the development of industry, the economic situation, as they find it, does not as yet offer to them the material conditions for the emancipation of the proletariat. They therefore search after a new social science, after new social laws, that are to create these conditions.

Historical action is to yield to their personal inventive action, historically created conditions of emancipation to fantastic ones, and the gradual, spontaneous class organization of the proletariat to an organization of society specially contrived by these inventors. Future history resolves itself, in their eyes, into the propaganda and the practical carrying out of their social plans.

In the formation of their plans they are conscious of caring chiefly for the interests of the working class, as being the most suf-

---

*Claude-Henri de Rouvroy, comte de Saint-Simon (1760–1825), a founder of Christian socialism. He proposed to organize society in accordance with his progressive social and economic theories, and prized science and the arts as vital elements of society. After his death, his French followers, the Saint-Simonians, tried to implement his theories, including that of each worker's compensation being based on his capabilities and contributions to the group.

†Charles Fourier (1772–1837), early French socialist; he proposed an idiosyncratic system of communal living based on production units known as phalanstères, or phalanges, in which members were compensated based on their phalange's overall productivity.

‡Robert Owen (1771–1858), British socialist, economist, and industrialist who created new communities of living and working based on his theories of labor and shared possession of the means of production.

fering class. Only from the point of view of being the most suffering class does the proletariat exist for them.

The undeveloped state of the class struggle, as well as their own surroundings, causes Socialists of this kind to consider themselves far superior to all class antagonisms. They want to improve the condition of every member of society, even that of the most favored. Hence, they habitually appeal to society at large, without distinction of class; nay, by preference, to the ruling class. For how can people, when once they understand their system, fail to see in it the best possible plan of the best possible state of society?

Hence, they reject all political, and especially all revolutionary action; they wish to attain their ends by peaceful means, and endeavor by small experiments, necessarily doomed to failure, and by the force of example to pave the way for the new social Gospel.

Such fantastic pictures of future society, painted at a time when the proletariat is still in a very undeveloped state and has but a fantastic conception of its own position, correspond with the first instinctive yearnings of that class for a general reconstruction of society.

But these Socialist and Communist publications contain also a critical element. They attack every principle of existing society. Hence they are full of the most valuable materials for the enlightenment of the working class. The practical measures proposed in them—such as the abolition of the distinction between town and country, of the family, of the carrying on of industries for the account of private individuals, and of the wage system; the proclamation of social harmony, the conversion of the functions of the State into a mere superintendence of productions—all these proposals point solely to the disappearance of class antagonisms which were at that time only just cropping up, and which in these publications are recognized in their earliest indistinct and undefined forms only. These proposals, therefore, are of a purely Utopian character.

The significance of Critical-Utopian Socialism and Communism bears an inverse relation to historical development. In proportion as the modern class struggle develops and takes definite shape, this fantastic standing apart from the contest, these fantastic attacks on it, lose all practical value and all theoretical justification. Therefore, although the originators of these systems were in many respects revolutionary, their disciples in every case have formed mere reactionary sects. They hold fast by the original views of their masters, in opposition to the progressive historical development of the proletariat. They, therefore, endeavor, and that consistently, to deaden the class struggle and to reconcile the class antagonisms. They still dream of experimental realization of their social Utopias, of founding isolated *"phalanstères,"* of establishing "Home Colonies," of setting up a "Little Icaria"*—duodecimo editions† of the New Jerusalem—and to realize all these castles in the air, they are compelled to appeal to the feelings and purses of the bourgeois. By degrees they sink into the category of the reactionary conservative Socialists depicted above, differing from these only by more systematic pedantry, and by their fanatical and superstitious belief in the miraculous effects of their social science.

They, therefore, violently oppose all political action on the part of the working class; such action, according to them, can only result from blind unbelief in the new Gospel.

The Owenites in England, and the Fourierists in France, respectively oppose the Chartists and the *Réformistes.*‡

---

*Phalanstères were Socialist colonies on the plan of Charles Fourier; Icaria was the name given by Cabet to his Utopia and, later on, to his American communist colony [Engels's note, 1888].

"Home colonies" were what Owen called his Communist model societies. Phalanstères was the name of the public palaces planned by Fourier. Icaria was the name given to the Utopian land of fancy, whose Communist institutions Cabet portrayed [Engels's note, 1890].

†Cheap editions of a text in a small format.

‡Reformers (French).

IV

Position of the Communists in Relation to the Various Existing Opposition Parties

SECTION II HAS MADE clear the relations of the Communists to the existing working-class parties, such as the Chartists* in England and the Agrarian Reformers† in America.

The Communists fight for the attainment of the immediate aims, for the enforcement of the momentary interests of the working class; but in the movement of the present, they also represent and take care of the future of that movement. In France the Communists ally themselves with the Social-Democrats‡ against the conservative and radical bourgeoisie, reserving, however, the right to take up a critical position in regard to phrases and illusions traditionally handed down from the great Revolution.

In Switzerland they support the Radicals, without losing sight of the fact that this party consists of antagonistic elements, partly of Democratic Socialists, in the French sense, partly of radical bourgeois.

In Poland they support the party that insists on an agrarian rev-

---

*Members of the first mass British working-class movement; active in the mid-nineteenth century, they demanded universal male suffrage, voting by secret ballot, and other democratic measures, many of which were ultimately adopted.

†Populist movement, active in the western and southern United States in the nineteenth and early twentieth centuries, that demanded government ownership of railroads and other measures to strengthen agriculture through government intervention.

‡The party then represented in Parliament by Ledru-Rollin, in literature by Louis Blanc, in the daily press by La Réforme. The name of Social-Democracy signified, with these its inventors, a section of the Democratic or Republican party more or less tinged with socialism [Engels's note, 1888].

The party in France which at that time called itself Socialist-Democratic was represented in political life by Ledru-Rollin and in literature by Louis Blanc; thus it differed immeasurably from present-day German Social-Democracy [Engels's note, 1890].

olution as the prime condition for national emancipation, that party which fomented the insurrection of Cracow in 1846.*

In Germany they fight with the bourgeoisie whenever it acts in a revolutionary way, against the absolute monarchy, the feudal squirearchy, and the petty bourgeoisie.

But they never cease, for a single instant, to instill into the working class the clearest possible recognition of the hostile antagonism between bourgeoisie and proletariat in order that the German workers may straightway use, as so many weapons against the bourgeoisie, the social and political conditions that the bourgeoisie must necessarily introduce along with its supremacy, and in order that after the fall of the reactionary classes in Germany the fight against the bourgeoisie itself may immediately begin.

The Communists turn their attention chiefly to Germany, because that country is on the eve of a bourgeois revolution that is bound to be carried out under more advanced conditions of European civilization, and with a much more developed proletariat than that of England in the 17th, and of France in the 18th century, and because the bourgeois revolution in Germany will be but the prelude to an immediately following proletarian revolution.

In short, the Communists everywhere support every revolutionary movement against the existing social and political order of things.

In all these movements they bring to the front, as the leading question in each, the property question, no matter what its degree of development at the time.

Finally, they labor everywhere for the union and agreement of the democratic parties of all countries.

The Communists disdain to conceal their views and aims. They openly declare that their ends can be attained only by the forcible overthrow of all existing social conditions. Let the ruling classes tremble at a Communistic revolution. The proletarians have nothing to lose but their chains. They have a world to win.

WORKING MEN OF ALL COUNTRIES, UNITE!

---

*Insurrection in Galicia (Austrian-controlled Poland) that Austria blamed on the free Republic of Cracow (also spelled Krakow); using the uprising as an excuse. Austria occupied and annexed Cracow with the consent of Russia and Prussia.

PREFACES to the MANIFESTO of the COMMUNIST PARTY

Karl Marx
Friedrich Engels

German Edition of 1872

The Communist League, an international association of workers, which could of course be only a secret one under the conditions obtaining at the time, commissioned the undersigned, at the Congress held in London in November 1847, to draw up for publication a detailed theoretical and practical program of the Party. Such was the origin of the following *Manifesto*, the manuscript of which traveled to London, to be printed a few weeks before the February Revolution. First published in German, it has been republished in that language in at least twelve different editions in Germany, England and America. It was published in English for the first time in 1850 in the *Red Republican*, London, translated by Miss Helen Macfarlane, and in 1871 in at least three different translations in America. A French version first appeared in Paris shortly before the June insurrection of 1848 and recently in *Le Socialiste* of New York. A new translation is in the course of preparation. A Polish version appeared in London shortly after it was first published in German. A Russian translation was published in Geneva in the sixties. Into Danish, too, it was translated shortly after its first appearance.

However much the state of things may have altered during the last twenty-five years, the general principles laid down in this *Manifesto* are, on the whole, as correct today as ever. Here and there some detail might be improved. The practical application of the principles will depend, as the *Manifesto* itself states, everywhere and at all times on the historical conditions for the time being existing, and for that reason no special stress is laid on the revolutionary measures proposed at the end of Section II. That passage would, in many respects, be very differently worded today. In view of the gigantic strides of Modern Industry in the last twenty-five years, and of the accompanying improved and extended party organization of the working class, in view of the practical experience gained, first in the February Revolution, and then still more in the Paris Commune, where the proletariat for the first time held political power for two whole months, this program has in some details become antiquated. One thing especially was proved by the Commune, viz., that "the working class cannot simply lay hold of the ready-made state machinery, and wield it for its own purposes." (See *The Civil War in France; Address of the General Council of the International Working Men's Asso-*

ciation, London, Truelove, 1871, p. 15, where this point is further developed.) Further, it is self-evident that the criticism of Socialist literature is deficient in relation to the present time because it comes down only to 1847; also, that the remarks on the relation of the Communists to the various opposition parties (Section IV), although in principle still correct, yet in practice are antiquated because the political situation has been entirely changed, and the progress of history has swept from off the earth the greater portion of the political parties there enumerated.

But, then, the *Manifesto* has become a historical document which we have no longer any right to alter. A subsequent edition may perhaps appear with an introduction bridging the gap from 1847 to the present day; this reprint was too unexpected to leave us time for that.

London, June 24, 1872
KARL MARX
FRIEDERICK ENGELS

Russian Edition of 1882

The first Russian edition of the *Manifesto of the Communist Party,* translated by Bakunin, was published early in the sixties by the printing office of the *Kolokol.* Then the West could see in it (the *Russian* edition of the *Manifesto*) only a literary curiosity. Such a view would be impossible today.

What a limited field the proletarian movement still occupied at that time (December 1847) is most clearly shown by the last section of the *Manifesto:* the position of the Communists in relation to the various opposition parties in the various countries. Precisely Russia and the United States are missing here. It was the time when Russia constituted the last great reserve of all European reaction, when the United States absorbed the surplus proletarian forces of Europe through immigration. Both countries provided Europe with raw materials and were at the same time markets for the sale of its industrial products. At that time both were, therefore, in one way or another pillars of the existing European order.

How very different today! Precisely European immigration fitted North America for a gigantic agricultural production, whose competition is shaking the very foundations of European landed property, large and small. In addition it enabled the United States to exploit its tremendous industrial resources with an energy and on a scale that must shortly break the industrial monopoly of Western Europe, and especially of England, existing up to now. Both circumstances react in revolutionary manner upon America itself. Step by step the small and middle landownership of the farmers, the basis of the whole political constitution, is succumbing to the competition of giant farms; simultaneously, a mass proletariat and a fabulous concentration of capitals are developing for the first time in the industrial regions.

And now Russia? During the Revolution of 1848–49 not only the European princes, but the European bourgeois as well, found their only salvation from the proletariat, just beginning to awaken, in Russian intervention. The Tsar was proclaimed the chief of European reaction. Today he is a prisoner of war of the revolution, in Gatchina,* and Russia forms the vanguard of revolutionary action in Europe.

The *Communist Manifesto* had as its object the proclamation of the inevitably impending dissolution of modern bourgeois property. But in Russia we find, face to face with the rapidly developing capitalist swindle and bourgeois landed property, just beginning to develop, more than half the land owned in common by the peasants. Now the question is: can the Russian *obshchina*,† though greatly undermined, yet a form of the primeval common ownership of land, pass directly to the higher form of communist common ownership? Or on the contrary, must it first pass through the same process of dissolution as constitutes the historical evolution of the West?

The only answer to that possible today is this: If the Russian Revolution becomes the signal for a proletarian revolution in the West, so that both complement each other, the present Russian common ownership of land may serve as the starting point for a communist development.

London, January 21, 1882
KARL MARX
FRIEDERICK ENGELS

---

*Town southwest of St. Petersburg.
†Type of Russian peasant commune, established around 1500, in which land was periodically redistributed according to each family's needs.

German Edition of 1883

The preface to the present edition I must, alas, sign alone. Marx, the man to whom the whole working class of Europe and America owes more than to anyone else, rests at Highgate Cemetery and over his grave the first grass is already growing. Since his death, there can be even less thought of revising or supplementing the *Manifesto*. All the more do I consider it necessary again to state here the following expressly:

The basic thought running through the *Manifesto*—that economic production and the structure of society of every historical epoch necessarily arising therefrom constitute the foundation for the political and intellectual history of that epoch; that consequently (ever since the dissolution of the primeval communal ownership of land) all history has been a history of class struggles, of struggles between exploited and exploiting, between dominated and dominating classes at various stages of social development; that this struggle, however, has now reached a stage where the exploited and oppressed class (the proletariat) can no longer emancipate itself from the class which exploits and oppresses it (the bourgeoisie), without at the same time for ever freeing the whole of society from exploitation, oppression and class struggles—this basic thought belongs solely and exclusively to Marx.*

I have already stated this many times; but precisely now it is necessary that it also stand in front of the *Manifesto* itself.

London, June 28, 1883
F. ENGELS

English Edition of 1888

The *Manifesto* was published as the platform of the Communist League, a workingmen's association, first exclusively German, later

---

*"This proposition," I wrote in the preface to the English translation, "which, in my opinion, is destined to do for history what Darwin's theory has done for biology, we, both of us, had been gradually approaching for some years before 1845. How far I had independently progressed toward it, is best shown by my Condition of the Working Class in England. But when I again met Marx at Brussels in spring, 1845, he had it ready worked out, and put it before me in terms almost as clear as those in which I have stated it here" [Engels's note, 1890].

on international, and under the political conditions of the Continent before 1848 unavoidably a secret society. At a Congress of the League, held in London in November 1847, Marx and Engels were commissioned to prepare for publication a complete theoretical and practical party program. Drawn up in German, in January 1848, the manuscript was sent to the printer in London a few weeks before the French revolution of February 24. A French translation was brought out in Paris, shortly before the insurrection of June 1848. The first English translation, by Miss Helen Macfarlane, appeared in George Julian Harney's *Red Republican,* London, 1850. A Danish and a Polish edition had also been published.

The defeat of the Parisian insurrection of June 1848—the first great battle between Proletariat and Bourgeoisie—drove again into the background, for a time, the social and political aspirations of the European working class. Thenceforth, the struggle for supremacy was again, as it had been before the revolution of February, solely between different sections of the propertied class; the working class was reduced to a fight for political elbow-room, and to the position of extreme wing of the middle-class Radicals. Wherever independent proletarian movements continued to show signs of life, they were ruthlessly hunted down. Thus the Prussian police hunted out the Central Board of the Communist League, then located in Cologne. The members were arrested and, after eighteen months' imprisonment, they were tried in October 1852. This celebrated "Cologne Communist trial" lasted from October 4 till November 12; seven of the prisoners were sentenced to terms of imprisonment in a fortress, varying from three to six years. Immediately after the sentence, the League was formally dissolved by the remaining members. As to the *Manifesto,* it seemed thenceforth to be doomed to oblivion.

When the European working class had recovered sufficient strength for another attack on the ruling classes, the International Working Men's Association sprang up. But this association, formed with the express aim of welding into one body the whole militant proletariat of Europe and America, could not at once proclaim the principles laid down in the *Manifesto.* The International was bound to have a program broad enough to be acceptable to the English Trades' Unions, to the followers of Proudhon in France, Belgium,

Italy and Spain, and to the Lassalleans* in Germany. Marx, who drew up this program to the satisfaction of all parties, entirely trusted to the intellectual development of the working class which was sure to result from combined action and mutual discussion. The very events and vicissitudes of the struggle against Capital, the defeats even more than the victories, could not help bringing home to men's minds the insufficiency of their various favorite nostrums, and preparing the way for a more complete insight into the true conditions of working-class emancipation. And Marx was right. The International, on its breaking up in 1874, left the workers quite different men from what it had found them in 1864. Proudhonism in France, Lassalleanism in Germany were dying out, and even the Conservative English Trades' Unions, though most of them had long since severed their connection with the International, were gradually advancing toward that point at which, last year at Swansea, their President could say in their name, "Continental Socialism has lost its terrors for us." In fact, the principles of the *Manifesto* had made considerable headway among the working men of all countries.

The *Manifesto* itself thus came to the front again. The German text had been, since 1850, reprinted several times in Switzerland, England and America. In 1872, it was translated into English in New York, where the translation was published in *Woodhull and Claflin's Weekly*. From this English version, a French one was made in *Le Socialiste* of New York. Since then at least two more English translations, more or less mutilated, have been brought out in America, and one of them has been reprinted in England. The first Russian translation, made by Bakunin, was published at Herzen's *Kolokol* office in Geneva, about 1863; a second one, by the heroic Vera Zasulich, also in Geneva, 1882. A new Danish edition is to be found in *Socialdemokratisk Bibliothek*, Copenhagen, 1885; a fresh French translation in *Le Socialiste*, Paris, 1885. From this latter a Spanish version was prepared and published in Madrid, 1886. Not counting the Ger-

---

*Lassalle personally, to us, always acknowledged himself to be a disciple of Marx, and, as such, stood on the ground of the Manifesto. But in his public agitation, 1862–64, he did not go beyond demanding cooperative workshops supported by state credit [Engels's note]. Lassalleans were followers of Ferdinand Lassalle (1825–1864), socialist thinker and economist; he established the iron law of wages, according to which wages fall to the lowest possible level.

man reprints, there have been at least twelve editions. An Armenian translation, which was to be published in Constantinople some months ago, did not see the light, I am told, because the publisher was afraid of bringing out a book with the name of Marx on it, while the translator declined to call it his own production. Of further translations into other languages I have heard, but have not seen them. Thus the history of the *Manifesto* reflects to a great extent the history of the modern working-class movement; at present it is undoubtedly the most widespread, the most international production of all Socialist literature, the common platform acknowledged by millions of workingmen from Siberia to California.

Yet, when it was written we could not have called it a *Socialist* Manifesto. By Socialists, in 1847, were understood, on the one hand, the adherents of the various utopian systems: Owenites in England, Fourierists in France, both of them already reduced to the position of mere sects, and gradually dying out; on the other hand, the most multifarious social quacks, who by all manners of tinkering professed to redress, without any danger to capital and profit, all sorts of social grievances, in both cases men outside the working-class movement and looking rather to the "educated" classes for support. Whatever portion of the working class had become convinced of the insufficiency of mere political revolutions and had proclaimed the necessity of a total social change, that portion then called itself Communist. It was a crude, rough-hewn, purely instinctive sort of Communism; still, it touched the cardinal point and was powerful enough amongst the working class to produce the Utopian Communism in France of Cabet,* and in Germany of Weitling.† Thus in 1847 Socialism was a middle-class movement, Communism a working-class movement. Socialism was, on the Continent at least, "respectable"; Communism was the very opposite. And as our notion from the very beginning was that "the emancipation of the working class must be the act of the working class itself," there could

---

*Etienne Cabet (1788–1856), French socialist and author of utopian novels, including *Voyage to Icaria*; he and his followers established several utopian communities in the United States.
†Wilhelm Weitling (1808–1871), early German socialist thinker who in 1838 organized the League of the Just, the predecessor of the Communist League.

be no doubt as to which of the two names we must take. Moreover, we have, ever since, been far from repudiating it.

The *Manifesto* being our joint production, I consider myself bound to state that the fundamental proposition which forms its nucleus belongs to Marx. That proposition is: that in every historical epoch, the prevailing mode of economic production and exchange, and the social organization necessarily following from it, form the basis upon which is built up, and from which alone can be explained, the political and intellectual history of that epoch; that consequently the whole history of mankind (since the dissolution of primitive tribal society, holding land in common ownership) has been a history of class struggles, contests between exploiting and exploited, ruling and oppressed classes; that the history of these class struggles forms a series of evolutions in which, nowadays, a stage has been reached where the exploited and oppressed class—the proletariat—cannot attain its emancipation from the sway of the exploiting and ruling class—the bourgeoisie—without at the same time, and once and for all, emancipating society at large from all exploitation, oppression, class distinctions and class struggles.

This proposition which, in my opinion, is destined to do for history what Darwin's theory has done for biology, we, both of us, had been gradually approaching for some years before 1845. How far I had independently progressed toward it, is best shown by my *Condition of the Working Class in England*. But when I again met Marx at Brussels, in spring, 1845, he had it ready worked out, and put it before me in terms almost as clear as those in which I have stated it here.

From our joint preface to the German edition of 1872, I quote the following:

[*Here Engels quotes the second paragraph and the first sentence of the third paragraph of this preface, see above. Then he continues:*]

The present translation is by Mr. Samuel Moore, the translator of the greater portion of Marx's *Capital*. We have revised it in common, and I have added a few notes explanatory of historical allusions.

London, January 30, 1888
FRIEDERICK ENGELS

German Edition of 1890

Since the above was written, a new German edition of the *Manifesto* has again become necessary, and much has also happened to the *Manifesto* which should be recorded here.

A second Russian translation—by Vera Zasulich—appeared at Geneva in 1882; the preface to that edition was written by Marx and myself. Unfortunately, the original German manuscript has gone astray; I must therefore retranslate from the Russian, which will in no way improve the text. It reads:

[*Here Engels quotes the preface to this edition, see above. Then he continues:*]

At about the same date, a new Polish version appeared in Geneva, *Manifest Komunistyczny.*

Furthermore, a new Danish translation has appeared in the *Social-demokratisk Bibliothek*, Kjöbenhavn, 1885. Unfortunately it is not quite complete; certain essential passages, which seem to have presented difficulties to the translator, have been omitted, and in addition there are signs of carelessness here and there, which are all the more unpleasantly conspicuous since the translation indicates that had the translator taken a little more pains he would have done an excellent piece of work.

A new French version appeared in 1885 in *Le Socialiste* of Paris; it is the best published to date.

From this latter a Spanish version was published the same year, first in *El Socialista* of Madrid, and then reissued in pamphlet form: *Manifiesto del Partido Comunista* por Carlos Marx y F. Engels, Madrid, Administración de *El Socialista*, Hernán Cortés 8.

As a matter of curiosity I may also mention that in 1887 the manuscript of an Armenian translation was offered to a publisher in Constantinople. But the good man did not have the courage to publish something bearing the name of Marx and suggested that the translator set down his own name as author, which the latter, however, declined.

After one and then another of the more or less inaccurate American translations had been repeatedly reprinted in England, an authentic version at last appeared in 1888. This was by my friend Samuel Moore, and we went through it together once more before it was sent to press. It is entitled: *Manifesto of the Communist Party*, by

Karl Marx and Frederick Engels. Authorized English Translation, edited and annotated by Frederick Engels. 1888. London, William Reeves, 185 Fleet st., E. C. I have added some of the notes of that edition to the present one.

The *Manifesto* has had a history of its own. Greeted with enthusiasm at the time of its appearance by the then still not at all numerous vanguard of scientific Socialism (as it proved by the translations mentioned in the first preface), it was soon forced into the background by the reaction that began with the defeat of the Paris workers in June 1848, and was finally excommunicated "according to law" by the conviction of the Cologne Communists in November 1852. With the disappearance from the public scene of the workers' movement that had begun with the February Revolution, the *Manifesto* too passed into the background.

When the working class of Europe had again gathered sufficient strength for a new onslaught upon the power of the ruling classes, the International Working Men's Association came into being. Its aim was to weld together into *one* huge army the whole militant working class of Europe and America. Therefore it could not *set out* from the principles laid down in the *Manifesto*. It was bound to have a program which would not shut the door on the English trade unions, the French, Belgian, Italian and Spanish Proudhonists and the German Lassalleans.* This program—the preamble to the Rules of the International—was drawn up by Marx with a master hand acknowledged even by Bakunin and the Anarchists. For the ultimate triumph of the ideas set forth in the *Manifesto* Marx relied solely and exclusively upon the intellectual development of the working class, as it necessarily had to ensue from united action and discussion. The events and vicissitudes in the struggle against capital, the defeats even more than the successes, could not but demonstrate to the fighters the inadequacy hitherto of their universal panaceas and make their minds more receptive to a thorough understanding of

---

*Lassalle personally, to us, always acknowledged himself to be a "disciple" of Marx, and, as such, stood, of course, on the ground of the Manifesto. Matters were quite different with regard to those of his followers who did not go beyond his demand for producers' cooperatives supported by state credits and who divided the whole working class into supporters of state assistance and supporters of self-assistance [Engels's note].

the true conditions for the emancipation of the workers. And Marx was right. The working class of 1874, at the dissolution of the International, was altogether different from that of 1864, at its foundation. Proudhonism in the Latin countries and the specific Lassalleanism in Germany were dying out, and even the then arch-conservative English trade unions were gradually approaching the point where in 1887 the chairman of their Swansea Congress could say in their name, "Continental Socialism has lost its terrors for us." Yet by 1887 Continental Socialism was almost exclusively the theory heralded in the *Manifesto*. Thus, to a certain extent, the history of the *Manifesto* reflects the history of the modern working-class movement since 1848. At present it is doubtless the most widely circulated, the most international product of all Socialist literature, the common program of many millions of workers of all countries, from Siberia to California.

Nevertheless, when it appeared we could not have called it a *Socialist* Manifesto. In 1847 two kinds of people were considered Socialists. On the one hand were the adherents of the various Utopian systems, notably the Owenites in England and the Fourierists in France, both of whom at that date had already dwindled to mere sects gradually dying out. On the other, the manifold types of social quacks who wanted to eliminate social abuses through their various universal panaceas and all kinds of patchwork, without hurting capital and profit in the least. In both cases, people who stood outside the labor movement and who looked for support rather to the "educated" classes. The section of the working class, however, which demanded a radical reconstruction of society, convinced that mere political revolutions were not enough, then called itself *Communist.* It was still a rough-hewn, only instinctive, and frequently somewhat crude Communism. Yet it was powerful enough to bring into being two systems of Utopian Communism—in France the "Icarian" Communism of Cabet, and in Germany that of Weitling. Socialism in 1847 signified a bourgeois movement, Communism, a working-class movement. Socialism was, on the Continent at least, quite respectable, whereas Communism was the very opposite. And since we were very decidedly of the opinion as early as then that "the emancipation of the workers must be the act of the working class itself," we could have no hesitation as to which of the two names we should choose. Nor has it ever occurred to us since to repudiate it.

"Working men of all countries, unite!" But few voices responded when we proclaimed these words to the world forty-two years ago, on the eve of the first Paris Revolution in which the proletariat came out with demands of its own. On September 28, 1864, however, the proletarians of most of the Western European countries joined hands in the International Working Men's Association of glorious memory. True, the International itself lived only nine years. But that the eternal union of the proletarians of all countries created by it is still alive and lives stronger than ever, there is no better witness than this day. Because today, as I write these lines, the European and American proletariat is reviewing its fighting forces, mobilized for the first time, mobilized as *one* army, under *one* flag, for *one* immediate aim: the standard eight-hour working day, to be established by legal enactment, as proclaimed by the Geneva Congress of the International in 1866, and again by the Paris Workers' Congress in 1889. And today's spectacle will open the eyes of the capitalists and landlords of all countries to the fact that today the working men of all countries are united indeed.

If only Marx were still by my side to see this with his own eyes!

London, May 1, 1890
F. ENGELS

Polish Edition of 1892

The fact that a new Polish edition of the *Communist Manifesto* has become necessary gives rise to various thoughts.

First of all, it is noteworthy that of late the *Manifesto* has become an index, as it were, of the development of large-scale industry on the European continent. In proportion as large-scale industry expands in a given country, the demand grows among the workers of that country for enlightenment regarding their position as the working class in relation to the possessing classes, the socialist movement spreads among them and the demand for the *Manifesto* increases. Thus, not only the state of the labor movement but also the degree of development of large-scale industry can be measured with fair accuracy in every country by the number of copies of the *Manifesto* circulated in the language of that country.

Accordingly, the new Polish edition indicates a decided progress of Polish industry. And there can be no doubt whatever that this progress since the previous edition published ten years ago has actually taken place. Russian Poland, Congress Poland, has become the big industrial region of the Russian Empire. Whereas Russian large-scale industry is scattered sporadically—a part around the Gulf of Finland, another in the center (Moscow and Vladimir), a third along the coasts of the Black and Azov seas, and still others elsewhere—Polish industry has been packed into a relatively small area and enjoys both the advantages and the disadvantages arising from such concentration. The competing Russian manufacturers acknowledged the advantages when they demanded protective tariffs against Poland, in spite of their ardent desire to transform the Poles into Russians. The disadvantages—for the Polish manufacturers and the Russian government—are manifest in the rapid spread of socialist ideas among the Polish workers and in the growing demand for the *Manifesto*.

But the rapid development of Polish industry, outstripping that of Russia, is in its turn a new proof of the inexhaustible vitality of the Polish people and a new guarantee of its impending national restoration. And the restoration of an independent strong Poland is a matter which concerns not only the Poles but all of us. A sincere international collaboration of the European nations is possible only if each of these nations is fully autonomous in its own house. The Revolution of 1848, which under the banner of the proletariat, after all, merely let the proletarian fighters do the work of the bourgeoisie, also secured the independence of Italy, Germany and Hungary through its testamentary executors, Louis Bonaparte and Bismarck; but Poland, which since 1792 had done more for the Revolution than all these three together, was left to its own resources when it succumbed in 1863 to a tenfold greater Russian force. The nobility could neither maintain nor regain Polish independence; today, to the bourgeoisie, this independence is, to say the least, immaterial. Nevertheless, it is a necessity for the harmonious collaboration of the European nations. It can be gained only by the young Polish proletariat, and in its hands it is secure. For the workers of all the rest of

Europe need the independence of Poland just as much as the Polish workers themselves.

London, February 10, 1892
F. ENGELS

Italian Edition of 1893

TO THE ITALIAN READER

Publication of the *Manifesto of the Communist Party* coincided, one may say, with March 18, 1848, the day of the revolutions in Milan and Berlin, which were armed uprisings of the two nations situated in the center, the one, of the continent of Europe, the other of the Mediterranean; two nations until then enfeebled by division and internal strife and thus fallen under foreign domination. While Italy was subject to the Emperor of Austria, Germany underwent the yoke, not less effective though more indirect, of the Tsar of all the Russias. The consequences of March 18, 1848 freed both Italy and Germany from this disgrace; if from 1848 to 1871 these two great nations were reconstituted and somehow again put on their own, it was, as Karl Marx used to say, because the men who suppressed the Revolution of 1848 were, nevertheless, its testamentary executors in spite of themselves.

Everywhere that revolution was the work of the working class; it was the latter that built the barricades and paid with its life-blood. Only the Paris workers, in overthrowing the government, had the very definite intention of overthrowing the bourgeois regime. But conscious though they were of the fatal antagonism existing between their own class and the bourgeoisie, still neither the economic progress of the country nor the intellectual development of the mass of French workers had as yet reached the stage which would have made a social reconstruction possible. In the final analysis, therefore, the fruits of the revolution were reaped by the capitalist class. In the other countries, in Italy, in Germany, in Austria, the workers from the very outset did nothing but raise the bourgeoisie to power. But in any country the rule of the bourgeoisie is impossible without national independence. Therefore, the Revolution of 1848 had to bring in its train the unity and autonomy of the nations that had lacked them up to then: Italy, Germany, Hungary. Poland will follow in turn.

Thus, if the Revolution of 1848 was not a socialist revolution, it paved the way, prepared the ground for the latter. Through the impetus given to large-scale industry in all countries, the bourgeois regime during the last forty-five years has everywhere created a numerous, concentrated and powerful proletariat. It has thus raised, to use the language of the *Manifesto,* its own grave-diggers. Without restoring autonomy and unity to each nation, it will be impossible to achieve the international union of the proletariat, or the peaceful and intelligent cooperation of these nations toward common aims. Just imagine joint international action by the Italian, Hungarian, German, Polish and Russian workers under the political conditions preceding 1848!

The battles fought in 1848 were thus not fought in vain. Nor have the forty-five years separating us from that revolutionary epoch passed to no purpose. The fruits are ripening, and all I wish is that the publication of this Italian translation may augur as well for the victory of the Italian proletariat as the publication of the original did for the international revolution.

The *Manifesto* does full justice to the revolutionary part played by capitalism in the past. The first capitalist nation was Italy. The close of the feudal Middle Ages and the opening of the modern capitalist era are marked by a colossal figure: an Italian, Dante, both the last poet of the Middle Ages and the first poet of modern times. Today, as in 1300, a new historical era is approaching. Will Italy give us the new Dante, who will mark the hour of birth of this new, proletarian era?

London, February 1, 1893
FRIEDRICH ENGELS

THE EIGHTEENTH BRUMAIRE OF LOUIS BONAPARTE

KARL MARX

I

HEGEL REMARKS SOMEWHERE THAT all facts and personages of great importance in world history occur, as it were, twice. He forgot to add: the first time as tragedy, the second as farce. Caussidière for Danton, Louis Blanc for Robespierre, the *Montagne* of 1848 to 1851 for the *Montagne* of 1793 to 1795, the Nephew for the Uncle. And the same caricature occurs in the circumstances attending the second edition of the eighteenth Brumaire!

Men make their own history, but they do not make it just as they please; they do not make it under circumstances chosen by themselves, but under circumstances directly encountered, given and transmitted from the past. The tradition of all the dead generations weighs like a nightmare on the brain of the living. And just when they seem engaged in revolutionizing themselves and things, in creating something that has never yet existed, precisely in such periods of revolutionary crisis they anxiously conjure up the spirits of the past to their service and borrow from them names, battle cries and costumes in order to present the new scene of world history in this time-honoured disguise and this borrowed language. Thus Luther donned the mask of the Apostle Paul, the Revolution of 1789 to 1814 draped itself alternately as the Roman republic and the Roman empire, and the Revolution of 1848 knew nothing better to do than to parody, now 1789, now the revolutionary tradition of 1793 to 1795. In like manner a beginner who has learnt a new language always translates it back into his mother tongue, but he has assimilated the spirit of the new language and can freely express himself in it only when he finds his way in it without recalling the old and forgets his native tongue in the use of the new.

Consideration of this conjuring up of the dead of world history reveals at once a salient difference. Camille Desmoulins, Danton, Robespierre, Saint-Just, Napoleon, the heroes as well as the parties and the masses of the old French Revolution, performed the task of their time in Roman costume and with Roman phrases, the task of unchaining and setting up modern *bourgeois* society. The first ones knocked the feudal basis to pieces and mowed off the feudal heads which had grown on it. The other created inside France the conditions under which alone free competition could be developed, parcelled landed property exploited and the unchained industrial productive power of the nation employed; and beyond the French borders he everywhere swept the feudal institutions away, so far as was necessary to furnish bourgeois society in France with a suitable up-to-date environment on the European Continent. The new social formation once established, the antediluvian Colossi disappeared and with them resurrected Romanity—the Brutuses, Gracchi, Publicolas, the tribunes, the senators, and Caesar himself.* Bourgeois society in its sober reality had begotten its true interpreters and mouth-pieces in the Says, Cousins, Royer-Collards, Benjamin Constants and Guizots;† its real military leaders sat behind the office desks, and the hog-headed Louis XVIII was its political chief. Wholly absorbed in the production of wealth and in peaceful competitive struggle, it no longer comprehended that ghosts from the days of Rome had watched over its cradle. But unheroic as bourgeois society is, it nevertheless took heroism, sacrifice, terror, civil war and battles of peoples to bring it into being. And in the classically austere traditions of the Roman republic its gladiators found the ideals and the art forms, the self-deceptions that they needed in order to conceal from themselves the bourgeois limitations of the content of their struggles and to keep their enthusiasm on the high plane of the great historical tragedy. Similarly, at another stage of development, a century earlier, Cromwell‡ and the English people had borrowed

---

*Marx lists different Roman dynasties, such as the Gracchi, and political institutions, such as that of the tribune and the senator, that were used initially as models for the French Revolution of 1789.

†These figures were important proponents of the bourgeois revolution. *Jean-Baptiste Say* (1767–1832): French economist, known for Say's Law, which posits that supply creates its own demand. *Victor Cousin* (1792–1867): professor of philosophy who attacked empiricism. *Pierre-Paul Royer-Collard* (1763–1845): philosopher and statesman who advocated a constitutional monarchy. *Benjamin Constant* (1767–1830): political writer known for anti-Napoleonic tracts and his literary masterpiece, *Adolphe*. *François Guizot* (1787–1874): premier who was overthrown by the February Revolution of 1848.

‡Oliver Cromwell (1599–1658), leader of the parliamentary forces in the English Civil Wars; he became lord protector of the Commonwealth, instituting Puritan rule in the last years of his life.

speech, passions and illusions from the Old Testament for their bourgeois revolution. When the real aim had been achieved, when the bourgeois transformation of English society had been accomplished, Locke* supplanted Habakkuk.†

Thus the awakening of the dead in those revolutions served the purpose of glorifying the new struggles, not of parodying the old; of magnifying the given task in imagination, not of fleeing from its solution in reality; of finding once more the spirit of revolution, not of making its ghost walk about again.

From 1848 to 1851 only the ghost of the old revolution walked about, from Marrast, the *républicain en gants jaunes*,‡ who disguised himself as the old Bailly, down to the adventurer, who hides his commonplace repulsive features under the iron death mask of Napoleon. An entire people, which had imagined that by means of a revolution it had imparted to itself an accelerated power of motion, suddenly finds itself set back into a defunct epoch and, in order that no doubt as to the relapse may be possible, the old dates arise again, the old chronology, the old names, the old edicts, which had long become a subject of antiquarian erudition, and the old minions of the law, who had seemed long decayed. The nation feels like that mad Englishman in Bedlam§ who fancies that he lives in the times of the ancient Pharaohs and daily bemoans the hard labour that he must perform in the Ethiopian mines as a gold digger, immured in this subterranean prison, a dimly burning lamp fastened to his head, the overseer of the slaves behind him with a long whip, and at the exits a confused welter of barbarian mercenaries, who understand neither the forced labourers in the mines nor one another, since they speak no common language. "And all this is expected of me," sighs the mad Englishman, "of me, a free-born Briton, in order to make gold for the old Pharaohs."

---

*John Locke (1632–1704), British empiricist philosopher who helped initiate the Enlightenment.

†Biblical prophet.

‡Marie-François-Pascal Armand Marrast (1801–1852), editor of the republican *Le National*; he helped trigger the February Revolution of 1848 by calling for mass protests, but he soon sided with the anti-revolutionary opposition and defended the status quo. Marx derides him here as the *républicain en gants jaunes* (republican in kid gloves).

§Term for a mental institution, derived from the abbreviated "nickname" for the Bethlehem Royal Hospital, the first English institution for the mentally ill.

"In order to pay the debts of the Bonaparte family," sighs the French nation. The Englishman, so long as he was in his right mind, could not get rid of the fixed idea of making gold. The French, so long as they were engaged in revolution, could not get rid of the memory of Napoleon, as the election of December 10 proved. They hankered to return from the perils of revolution to the fleshpots of Egypt, and December 2, 1851 was the answer. They have not only a caricature of the old Napoleon, they have the old Napoleon himself, caricatured as he must appear in the middle of the nineteenth century.

The social revolution of the nineteenth century cannot draw its poetry from the past, but only from the future. It cannot begin with itself before it has stripped off all superstition in regard to the past. Earlier revolutions required recollections of past world history in order to drug themselves concerning their own content. In order to arrive at its own content, the revolution of the nineteenth century must let the dead bury their dead. There the phrase went beyond the content; here the content goes beyond the phrase.

The February Revolution was a surprise attack, a *taking* of the old society *unawares*, and the people proclaimed this unexpected *stroke* as a deed of world importance, ushering in a new epoch. On December 2 the February Revolution is conjured away by a card-sharper's trick, and what seems overthrown is no longer the monarchy but the liberal concessions that were wrung from it by centuries of struggle. Instead of *society* having conquered a new content for itself, it seems that the *state* only returned to its oldest form, to the shamelessly simple domination of the sabre and the cowl. This is the answer to the *coup de main** of February 1848, given by the *coup de tête*[†] of December 1851. Easy come, easy go. Meanwhile the interval of time has not passed by unused. During the years 1848 to 1851 French society has made up, and that by an abbreviated because revolutionary method, for the studies and experiences which, in a regular, so to speak, textbook course of development would have had to precede the February Revolution, if it was to be more than a ruffling of the surface. Society now seems to have fallen back behind its point of departure; it has in truth first to create for itself the rev-

---

*Surprise attack.
†Impulsive act.

olutionary point of departure, the situation, the relations, the conditions under which alone modern revolution becomes serious.

Bourgeois revolutions, like those of the eighteenth century, storm swiftly from success to success; their dramatic effects outdo each other; men and things seem set in sparkling brilliants; ecstasy is the everyday spirit; but they are short-lived; soon they have attained their zenith, and a long crapulent depression lays hold of society before it learns soberly to assimilate the results of its storm-and-stress period. On the other hand, proletarian revolutions, like those of the nineteenth century, criticize themselves constantly, interrupt themselves continually in their own course, come back to the apparently accomplished in order to begin it afresh, deride with unmerciful thoroughness the inadequacies, weaknesses and paltrinesses of their first attempts, seem to throw down their adversary only in order that he may draw new strength from the earth and rise again, more gigantic, before them, recoil ever and anon from the indefinite prodigiousness of their own aims, until a situation has been created which makes all turning back impossible, and the conditions themselves cry out:

> *Hic Rhodus, hic salta!*
> *Here is the rose, here dance!*

For the rest, every fairly competent observer, even if he had not followed the course of French developments step by step, must have had a presentiment that an unheard-of fiasco was in store for the revolution. It was enough to hear the self-complacent howl of victory with which Messieurs the Democrats congratulated each other on the expected gracious consequences of the second Sunday in May 1852. In their minds the second Sunday in May 1852 had become a fixed idea, a dogma, like the day on which Christ should reappear and the millennium begin, in the minds of the Chiliasts. As ever, weakness had taken refuge in a belief in miracles, fancied the enemy overcome when he was only conjured away in imagination, and it lost all understanding of the present in a passive glorification of the future that was in store for it and of the deeds it had *in petto** but which it merely did not want to carry out as yet. Those heroes who

---

*To have something *in petto* (Latin) means to have something up one's sleeve.

seek to disprove their demonstrated incapacity by mutually offering each other their sympathy and getting together in a crowd had tied up their bundles, collected their laurel wreaths in advance and were just then engaged in discounting on the exchange market the republics *in partibus* for which they had already providently organized the government personnel with all the calm of their unassuming disposition. December 2 struck them like a thunderbolt from a clear sky, and the peoples that in periods of pusillanimous depression gladly let their inward apprehension be drowned by the loudest bawlers will perchance have convinced themselves that the times are past when the cackle of geese could save the Capitol.

The Constitution, the National Assembly, the dynastic parties, the blue and the red republicans, the heroes of Africa, the thunder from the platform, the sheet lightning of the daily press, the entire literature, the political names and the intellectual reputations, the civil law and the penal code, the *liberté, égalité, fraternité* and the second Sunday in May 1852—all has vanished like a phantasmagoria before the spell of a man whom even his enemies do not make out to be a sorcerer. Universal suffrage seems to have survived only for a moment, in order that with its own hand it may make its last will and testament before the eyes of all the world and declare in the name of the people itself: All that exists deserves to perish.

It is not enough to say, as the French do, that their nation was taken unawares. A nation and a woman are not forgiven the unguarded hour in which the first adventurer that came along could violate them. The riddle is not solved by such turns of speech, but merely formulated differently. It remains to be explained how a nation of thirty-six millions can be surprised and delivered unresisting into captivity by three *chevaliers d'industrie.**

Let us recapitulate in general outline the phases that the French Revolution went through from February 24, 1848, to December 1851.

Three main periods are unmistakable: *the February period*; May 4, 1848, to May 28, 1849: *the period of the constitution of the republic, or of the Constituent National Assembly*; May 28, 1849, to December 2,

---

*Industrial leaders (French). Marx is referring to the industrial interests behind the February Revolution.

1851: *the period of the constitutional republic* or *of the Legislative National Assembly.*

The *first period,* from February 24, or the overthrow of Louis Philippe,* to May 4, 1848, the meeting of the Constituent Assembly, the *February period* proper, may be described as the *prologue* to the revolution. Its character was officially expressed in the fact that the government improvised by it itself declared that it was *provisional* and, like the government, everything that was mooted, attempted or enunciated during this period proclaimed itself to be only *provisional.* Nothing and nobody ventured to lay claim to the right of existence and of real action. All the elements that had prepared or determined the revolution, the dynastic opposition, the republican bourgeoisie, the democratic-republican petty bourgeoisie and the social-democratic workers, provisionally found their place in the February *government.*

It could not be otherwise. The February days originally intended an electoral reform, by which the circle of the politically privileged among the possessing class itself was to be widened and the exclusive domination of the aristocracy of finance overthrown. When it came to the actual conflict, however, when the people mounted the barricades, the National Guard maintained a passive attitude, the army offered no serious resistance and the monarchy ran away, the republic appeared to be a matter of course. Every party construed it in its own way. Having secured it arms in hand, the proletariat impressed its stamp upon it and proclaimed it to be a *social republic.* There was thus indicated the general content of the modern revolution, a content which was in most singular contradiction to everything that, with the material available, with the degree of education attained by the masses, under the given circumstances and relations, could be immediately realized in practice. On the other hand, the claims of all the remaining elements that had collaborated in the February Revolution were recognized by the lion's share that they obtained in the government. In no period do we, therefore, find a more confused mixture of high-flown phrases and actual uncer-

---

*Louis Philippe (1773–1850), who was king of France until he was forced to abdicate during the February Revolution of 1848.

tainty and clumsiness, of more enthusiastic striving for innovation and more deeply-rooted domination of the old routine, of more apparent harmony of the whole of society and more profound estrangement of its elements. While the Paris proletariat still revelled in the vision of the wide prospects that had opened before it and indulged in seriously-meant discussions on social problems, the old powers of society had grouped themselves, assembled, reflected and found unexpected support in the mass of the nation, the peasants and petty bourgeois, who all at once stormed on to the political stage, after the barriers of the July Monarchy* had fallen.

The *second period,* from May 4, 1848, to the end of May 1849, is the period of the *constitution,* the *foundation, of the bourgeois republic.* Directly after the February days not only had the dynastic opposition been surprised by the republicans and the republicans by the Socialists, but all France by Paris. The National Assembly, which met on May 4, 1848, had emerged from the national elections and represented the nation. It was a living protest against the pretensions of the February days and was to reduce the results of the revolution to the bourgeois scale. In vain the Paris proletariat, which immediately grasped the character of this National Assembly, attempted on May 15, a few days after it met, forcibly to negate its existence, to dissolve it, to disintegrate again into its constituent parts the organic form in which the proletariat was threatened by the reacting spirit of the nation. As is known, May 15 had no other result save that of removing Blanqui† and his comrades, that is, the real leaders of the proletarian party, from the public stage for the entire duration of the cycle we are considering.

The *bourgeois monarchy* of Louis Philippe can be followed only by a *bourgeois republic,* that is to say, whereas a limited section of the bourgeoisie ruled in the name of the king, the whole of the bourgeoisie will now rule in the name of the people. The demands of the Paris proletariat are utopian nonsense, to which an end must be

---

*Monarchy established by the July Revolution of 1830; it replaced the religious Charles X (1757–1836) with Louis Philippe (1773–1850).

†Louis-Auguste Blanqui (1805–1881), French revolutionary writer and activist in several secret societies. He was involved in all three revolutions in France during the nineteenth century: the Revolution of 1830, the February Revolution of 1848, and the Paris Commune of 1870.

put. To this declaration of the Constituent National Assembly the Paris proletariat replied with the *June Insurrection,* the most colossal event in the history of European civil wars. The bourgeois republic triumphed. On its side stood the aristocracy of finance, the industrial bourgeoisie, the middle class, the petty bourgeois, the army, the *lumpenproletariat** organized as the Mobile Guard, the intellectual lights, the clergy and the rural population. On the side of the Paris proletariat stood none but itself. More than three thousand insurgents were butchered after the victory, and fifteen thousand were transported without trial. With this defeat the proletariat passes into the *background* of the revolutionary stage. It attempts to press forward again on every occasion, as soon as the movement appears to make a fresh start, but with ever decreased expenditure of strength and always slighter results. As soon as one of the social strata situated above it gets into revolutionary ferment, the proletariat enters into an alliance with it and so shares all the defeats that the different parties suffer, one after another. But these subsequent blows become the weaker, the greater the surface of society over which they are distributed. The more important leaders of the proletariat in the Assembly and in the press successively fall victims to the courts, and ever more equivocal figures come to head it. In part it throws itself into *doctrinaire experiments, exchange banks and workers' associations, hence into a movement in which it renounces the revolutionizing of the old world by means of the latter's own great, combined resources, and seeks, rather, to achieve its salvation behind society's back, in private fashion, within its limited conditions of existence, and hence necessarily suffers shipwreck.* It seems to be unable either to rediscover revolutionary greatness in itself or to win new energy from the connections newly entered into, until *all classes* with which it contended in June themselves lie prostrate beside it. But at least it succumbs with the honours of the great, world-historic struggle; not only France, but all Europe trembles at the June earthquake, while the ensuing defeats of the upper classes are so cheaply bought that they require bare-faced exaggeration by the victorious party to be able to pass for events at all, and become

---

*Literally, the proletariat of rags (German); those at the margins of the working class, such as vagabonds and criminals.

the more ignominious the further the defeated party is removed from the proletarian party.

The defeat of the June insurgents, to be sure, had now prepared, had levelled the ground on which the bourgeois republic could be founded and built up, but it had shown at the same time that in Europe the questions at issue are other than that of "republic or monarchy." It had revealed that here *bourgeois republic* signifies the unlimited despotism of one class over other classes. It had proved that in countries with an old civilization, with a developed formation of classes, with modern conditions of production and with an intellectual consciousness in which all traditional ideas have been dissolved by the work of centuries, *the republic* signifies *in general only the political form of revolution of bourgeois society* and not its *conservative form of life*, as, for example, in the United States of North America, where, though classes already exist, they have not yet become fixed, but continually change and interchange their elements in constant flux, where the modern means of production, instead of coinciding with a stagnant surplus population, rather compensate for the relative deficiency of heads and hands, and where, finally, the feverish, youthful movement of material production, which has to make a new world its own, has left neither time nor opportunity for abolishing the old spirit world.

During the June days all classes and parties had united in the *party of Order* against the proletarian class as the *party of Anarchy*, of Socialism, of Communism. They had "saved" society from "*the enemies of society*." They had given out the watchwords of the old society, "*property, family, religion, order,*" to their army as passwords and had proclaimed to the counter-revolutionary crusaders: "In this sign thou shalt conquer!" From that moment, as soon as one of the numerous parties which had gathered under this sign against the June insurgents seeks to hold the revolutionary battlefield in its own class interest, it goes down before the cry: "Property, family, religion, order." Society is saved just as often as the circle of its rulers contracts, as a more exclusive interest is maintained against a wider one. Every demand of the simplest bourgeois financial reform, of the most ordinary liberalism, of the most formal republicanism, of the most shallow democracy, is simultaneously castigated as an "attempt on society" and stigmatized as "Socialism." And, finally, the high priests of "the religion and order" themselves are driven with kicks from their Pythian tripods,* hauled out of their beds in the darkness of night, put in prison-vans, thrown into dungeons or sent into exile; their temple is razed to the ground, their mouths are sealed, their pens broken, their law torn to pieces in the name of religion, of property, of the family, of order. Bourgeois fanatics for order are shot down on their balconies by mobs of drunken soldiers, their domestic sanctuaries profaned, their houses bombarded for amusement—in the name of property, of the family, of religion and of order. Finally, the scum of bourgeois society forms the *holy phalanx of order* and the hero Crapulinski installs himself in the Tuileries as the "*saviour of society.*"

---

*Seats of authority. The term comes from mythology and refers to the three-legged stool on which Pythia, the priestess of Apollo, sat when she uttered her oracle in the temple of Delphi.

II

LET US PICK UP the threads of the development once more.

The history of the *Constituent National Assembly* since the June days is the *history of the domination and the disintegration of the republican faction of the bourgeoisie,* of that faction which is known by the names of tricolour republicans, pure republicans, political republicans, formalist republicans, etc.

Under the bourgeois monarchy of Louis Philippe it had formed the *official* republican *opposition* and consequently a recognized component part of the political world of the day. It had its representatives in the Chambers and a considerable sphere of influence in the press. Its Paris organ, the *National,* was considered just as respectable in its way as the *Journal des Débats.* Its character corresponded to this position under the constitutional monarchy. It was not a faction of the bourgeoisie held together by great common interests and marked off by specific conditions of production. It was a clique of republican-minded bourgeois, writers, lawyers, officers and officials that owed its influence to the personal antipathies of the country against Louis Philippe, to memories of the old republic, to the republican faith of a number of enthusiasts, above all, however, to *French nationalism,* whose hatred of the Vienna treaties and of the alliance with England it stirred up perpetually. A large part of the following that the *National* had under Louis Philippe was due to this concealed imperialism, which could consequently confront it later, under the republic, as a deadly rival in the person of Louis Bonaparte. It fought the aristocracy of finance, as did all the rest of the bourgeois opposition. Polemics against the budget, which were closely connected in France with fighting the aristocracy of finance, procured popularity too cheaply and material for puritanical leading articles too plentifully, not to be exploited. The industrial bourgeoisie was grateful to it for its slavish defence of the French protectionist system, which it accepted, however, more on national grounds than on grounds of national economy; the bourgeoisie as a whole, for its vicious denunciation of Communism and Socialism.

74

For the rest, the party of the *National* was *purely republican,* that is, it demanded a republican instead of a monarchist form of bourgeois rule and, above all, the lion's share of this rule. Concerning the conditions of this transformation it was by no means clear in its own mind. On the other hand, what was clear as daylight to it and was publicly acknowledged at the reform banquets in the last days of Louis Philippe, was its unpopularity with the democratic petty bourgeois and, in particular, with the revolutionary proletariat. These pure republicans, as is, indeed, the way with pure republicans, were already on the point of contenting themselves in the first instance with a regency of the Duchess of Orleans, when the February Revolution broke out and assigned their best-known representatives a place in the Provisional Government. From the start, they naturally had the confidence of the bourgeoisie and a majority in the Constituent National Assembly. The *socialist* elements of the Provisional Government were excluded forthwith from the Executive Commission which the National Assembly formed when it met, and the party of the *National* took advantage of the outbreak of the June insurrection to discharge the *Executive Commission* also, and therewith to get rid of its closest rivals, the *petty-bourgeois,* or *democratic, republicans* (Ledru-Rollin, etc.). Cavaignac, the general of the bourgeois-republican party who commanded the June massacre, took the place of the Executive Commission with a sort of dictatorial power. Marrast, former editor-in-chief of the *National,* became the perpetual president of the Constituent National Assembly, and the ministries, as well as all other important posts, fell to the portion of the pure republicans.

The republican bourgeois faction, which had long regarded itself as the legitimate heir of the July Monarchy, thus found its fondest hopes exceeded; it attained power, however, not as it had dreamed under Louis Philippe, through a liberal revolt of the bourgeoisie against the throne, but through a rising of the proletariat against capital, a rising laid low with grape-shot. What it had conceived as the *most revolutionary* event turned out in reality to be the *most counter-revolutionary.* The fruit fell into its lap, but it fell from the tree of knowledge, not from the tree of life.

The exclusive *rule of the bourgeois republicans* lasted only from

June 24 to December 10, 1848. It is summed up in the *drafting of a republican constitution* and in the *state of siege of Paris.*

The new *Constitution* was at bottom only the republicanized edition of the constitutional Charter of 1830. The narrow electoral qualification of the July Monarchy, which excluded even a large part of the bourgeoisie from political rule, was incompatible with the existence of the bourgeois republic. In lieu of this qualification, the February Revolution had at once proclaimed direct universal suffrage. The bourgeois republicans could not undo this event. They had to content themselves with adding the limiting proviso of a six months' residence in the constituency. The old organization of the administration, of the municipal system, of the judicial system, of the army, etc., continued to exist inviolate, or, where the Constitution changed them, the change concerned the table of contents, not the contents; the name, not the subject matter.

The inevitable general staff of the liberties of 1848, personal liberty, liberty of the press, of speech, of association, of assembly, of education and religion, etc., received a constitutional uniform, which made them invulnerable. For each of these liberties is proclaimed as the *absolute* right of the French *citoyen,** but always with the marginal note that it is unlimited so far as it is not limited by the "*equal rights of others* and the *public safety*" or by "laws" which are intended to mediate just this harmony of the individual liberties with one another and with the public safety. For example: "The citizens have the right of association, of peaceful and unarmed assembly, of petition and of expressing their opinions, whether in the press or in any other way. *The enjoyment of these rights has no limit save the equal rights of others and the public safety.*" (Chapter II of the French Constitution, §8.)—"Education is free. Freedom of education shall be *enjoyed* under the conditions fixed by law and under the supreme control of the state." (*Ibidem,* §9.)—"The home of every citizen is inviolable *except* in the forms prescribed by law." (Chapter II, §3.) Etc., etc.—The Constitution, therefore, constantly refers to future *organic* laws which are to put into effect those marginal notes and regulate the enjoyment of these unrestricted liberties in such manner that they will collide neither with one another nor with the pub-

---

*Citizen (French).

lic safety. And later, these organic laws were brought into being by the friends of order and all those liberties regulated in such manner that the bourgeoisie in its enjoyment of them finds itself unhindered by the equal rights of the other classes. Where it forbids these liberties entirely to "the others" or permits enjoyment of them under conditions that are just so many police traps, this always happens solely in the interest of "*public safety,*" that is, the safety of the bourgeoisie, as the Constitution prescribes. In the sequel, both sides accordingly appeal with complete justice to the Constitution: the friends of order, who abrogated all these liberties, as well as the democrats, who demanded all of them. For each paragraph of the Constitution contains its own antithesis, its own Upper and Lower House, namely, liberty in the general phrase, abrogation of liberty in the marginal note. Thus, so long as the *name* of freedom was respected and only its actual realization prevented, of course in a legal way, the constitutional existence of liberty remained intact, inviolate, however mortal the blows dealt to its existence *in actual life.*

This Constitution, made inviolable in so ingenious a manner, was nevertheless, like Achilles, vulnerable in one point, not in the heel, but in the head, or rather in the two heads in which it wound up— the *Legislative Assembly,* on the one hand, the *President,* on the other. Glance through the Constitution and you will find that only the paragraphs in which the relationship of the President to the Legislative Assembly is defined are absolute, positive, non-contradictory, and cannot be distorted. For here it was a question of the bourgeois republicans safeguarding themselves. §§45-70 of the Constitution are so worded that the National Assembly can remove the President constitutionally, whereas the President can remove the National Assembly only unconstitutionally, only by setting aside the Constitution itself. Here, therefore, it challenges its forcible destruction. It not only sanctifies the division of powers, like the Charter of 1830, it widens it into an intolerable contradiction. The *play of the constitutional powers,* as Guizot termed the parliamentary squabble between the legislative and executive power, is in the Constitution of 1848 continually played *va-banque.** On one side are seven hundred and fifty representatives of the people, elected by universal suffrage

---

*Betting everything (French).

and eligible for re-election; they form an uncontrollable, indissoluble, indivisible National Assembly, a National Assembly that enjoys legislative omnipotence, decides in the last instance on war, peace and commercial treaties, alone possesses the right of amnesty and, by its permanence, perpetually holds the front of the stage. On the other side is the President, with all the attributes of royal power, with authority to appoint and dismiss his ministers independently of the National Assembly, with all the resources of the executive power in his hands, bestowing all posts and disposing thereby in France of the livelihoods of at least a million and a half people, for so many depend on the five hundred thousand officials and officers of every rank. He has the whole of the armed forces behind him. He enjoys the privilege of pardoning individual criminals, of suspending National Guards, of discharging, with the concurrence of the Council of State, general, cantonal and municipal councils elected by the citizens themselves. Initiative and direction are reserved to him in all treaties with foreign countries. While the Assembly constantly performs on the boards and is exposed to daily public criticism, he leads a secluded life in the Elysian Fields, and that with Article 45 of the Constitution before his eyes and in his heart, crying to him daily: "*Frère, il faut mourir!*" Your power ceases on the second Sunday of the lovely month of May in the fourth year after your election! Then your glory is at an end, the piece is not played twice and if you have debts, look to it betimes that you pay them off with the six hundred thousand francs granted you by the Constitution, unless, perchance, you should prefer to go to Clichy on the second Monday of the lovely month of May!—Thus, whereas the Constitution assigns actual power to the President, it seeks to secure moral power for the National Assembly. Apart from the fact that it is impossible to create a moral power by paragraphs of law, the Constitution here abrogates itself once more by having the President elected by all Frenchmen through direct suffrage. While the votes of France are split up among the seven hundred and fifty members of the National Assembly, they are here, on the contrary, concentrated on a single individual. While each separate representative of the people represents only this or that party, this or that town, this or that bridgehead, or even only the mere necessity of electing some one as the seven hundred and fiftieth, without examining too closely either the cause or the man, *he* is the elect of the nation and the act of his election is the trump that the sovereign people plays once every four years. The elected National Assembly stands in a metaphysical relation, but the elected President in a personal relation, to the nation. The National Assembly, indeed, exhibits in its individual representatives the manifold aspects of the national spirit, but in the President this national spirit finds its incarnation. As against the Assembly, he possesses a sort of divine right; he is President by the grace of the people.

Thetis, the sea goddess, had prophesied to Achilles that he would die in the bloom of youth. The Constitution, which, like Achilles, had its weak spot, had also, like Achilles, its presentiment that it must go to an early death. It was sufficient for the constitution-making pure republicans to cast a glance from the lofty heaven of their ideal republic at the profane world to perceive how the arrogance of the royalists, the Bonapartists, the Democrats, the Communists as well as their own discredit grew daily in the same measure as they approached the completion of their great legislative work of art, without Thetis on this account having to leave the sea and communicate the secret to them. They sought to cheat destiny by a catch in the Constitution, through §111 of it, according to which every motion for a *revision of the Constitution* must be supported by at least three-quarters of the votes, cast in three successive debates between which an entire month must always lie, with the added proviso that not less than five hundred members of the National Assembly must vote. Thereby they merely made the impotent attempt still to exercise a power—when only a parliamentary minority, as which they already saw themselves prophetically in their mind's eye—a power which at the present time, when they commanded a parliamentary majority and all the resources of governmental authority, was slipping daily more and more from their feeble hands.

Finally the Constitution, in a melodramatic paragraph, entrusts itself "to the vigilance and the patriotism of the whole French people and every single Frenchman," after it had previously entrusted in another paragraph the "vigilant" and "patriotic" to the tender, most painstaking care of the High Court of Justice, the *"haute cour,"* invented by it for the purpose.

Such was the Constitution of 1848, which on December 2, 1851, was not overthrown by a head, but fell down at the touch of a mere hat; this hat, to be sure, was a three-cornered Napoleonic hat.

While the bourgeois republicans in the Assembly were busy devising, discussing and voting this Constitution, Cavaignac* outside the Assembly maintained the *state of siege of Paris*. The state of siege of Paris was the midwife of the Constituent Assembly in its travail of republican creation. If the Constitution is subsequently put out of existence by bayonets, it must not be forgotten that it was likewise by bayonets, and these turned against the people, that it had to be protected in its mother's womb and by bayonets that it had to be brought into existence. The forefathers of the "respectable republicans" had sent their symbol, the tricolour, on a tour round Europe. They themselves in turn produced an invention that of itself made its way over the whole Continent, but returned to France with ever renewed love until it has now become naturalized in half her Departments—the *state of siege*. A splendid invention, periodically employed in every ensuing crisis in the course of the French Revolution. But barrack and bivouac, which were thus periodically laid on French society's head to compress its brain and render it quiet; sabre and musket, which were periodically allowed to act as judges and administrators, as guardians and censors, to play policeman and do night watchman's duty; moustache and uniform, which were periodically trumpeted forth as the highest wisdom of society and as its rector—were not barrack and bivouac, sabre and musket, moustache and uniform finally bound to hit upon the idea of rather saving society once and for all by proclaiming their own regime as the highest and freeing civil society completely from the trouble of governing itself? Barrack and bivouac, sabre and musket, moustache and uniform were bound to hit upon this idea all the more as they might then also expect better cash payment for their higher services, whereas from the merely periodical state of siege and the transient rescues of society at the bidding of this or that bourgeois faction little of substance was gleaned save some killed and wounded and some friendly bourgeois grimaces. Should not the military at last

---

*Louis Eugène Cavaignac (1802–1857), French general who was appointed minister of war in 1848; he suppressed the revolutionary workers by declaring a state of siege, which gave him dictatorial powers, and became known as "the butcher of June."

one day play state of siege in their own interest and for their own benefit, and at the same time besiege the citizens' purses? Moreover, be it noted in passing, one must not forget that *Colonel Bernard*, the same military commission president who under Cavaignac had 15,000 insurgents deported without trial, is at this moment again at the head of the military commissions active in Paris.

Whereas, with the state of siege in Paris, the respectable, the pure republicans planted the nursery in which the praetorians* of December 2, 1851 were to grow up, they on the other hand deserve praise for the reason that, instead of exaggerating the national sentiment as under Louis Philippe, they now, when they had command of the national power, crawled before foreign countries, and, instead of setting Italy free, let her be reconquered by Austrians and Neapolitans.[†] Louis Bonaparte's election as President on December 10, 1848, put an end to the dictatorship of Cavaignac and to the Constituent Assembly.

In §44 of the Constitution it is stated: "The President of the French Republic must never have lost his status of a French citizen." The first President of the French republic, L. N. Bonaparte, had not merely lost his status of a French citizen, had not only been an English special constable, he was even a naturalized Swiss.

I have worked out elsewhere the significance of the election of December 10.[‡] I will not revert to it here. It is sufficient to remark here that it was a *reaction of the peasants*, who had had to pay the costs of the February Revolution, against the remaining classes of the nation, a *reaction of the country against the town*. It met with great approval in the army, for which the republicans of the *National* had provided neither glory nor additional pay, among the big bourgeoisie, which hailed Bonaparte as a bridge to monarchy, among the proletarians and petty bourgeois, who hailed him as a scourge for Cavaignac. I shall have an opportunity later of going more closely into the relationship of the peasants to the French Revolution.

---

*Bodyguards of the Roman emperors.
†Marx refers to the fact that the Roman Republic, declared in 1849 by Giuseppe Mazzini (1805–1872), was quickly felled by the counter-revolutionary intervention of Austria, the Kingdom of Naples, and France.
‡See Karl Marx, *The Class Struggles in France, 1848–1850.*

The period from December 20, 1848, until the dissolution of the Constituent Assembly, in May 1849, comprises the history of the downfall of the bourgeois republicans. After having founded a republic for the bourgeoisie, driven the revolutionary proletariat out of the field and reduced the democratic petty bourgeoisie to silence for the time being, they are themselves thrust aside by the mass of the bourgeoisie, which justly impounds this republic as *its property*. This bourgeois mass was, however, *royalist*. One section of it, the large landowners, had ruled during the *Restoration* and was accordingly *Legitimist*.* The other, the aristocrats of finance and big industrialists, had ruled during the July Monarchy and was consequently *Orleanist*.† The high dignitaries of the army, the university, the church, the bar, the academy and of the press were to be found on either side, though in various proportions. Here, in the bourgeois republic, which bore neither the name *Bourbon* nor the name *Orleans*, but the name *Capital*, they had found the form of state in which they could rule *conjointly*. The June Insurrection had already united them in the "party of Order." Now it was necessary, in the first place, to remove the coterie of bourgeois republicans who still occupied the seats of the National Assembly. Just as brutal as these pure republicans had been in their misuse of physical force against the people, just as cowardly, mealy-mouthed, broken-spirited and incapable of fighting were they now in their retreat, when it was a question of maintaining their republicanism and their legislative rights against the executive power and the royalists. I need not relate here the ignominious history of their dissolution. They did not succumb; they passed out of existence. Their history has come to an end forever, and, both inside and outside the Assembly, they figure in the following period only as memories, memories that seem to regain life whenever the mere name of Republic is once more the issue and as often as the revolutionary conflict threatens to sink down to the lowest level. I may remark in passing that the journal which gave its name to this party, the *National*, was converted to Socialism in the following period.

---

*Type of royalist who demanded the return of the older branch of the Bourbon dynasty overthrown with King Charles X (1757–1836) in the Revolution of 1830.
†Type of royalist who supported the Orléans dynasty, which ruled as a constitutional monarchy between 1830 and 1848.

Before we finish with this period we must still cast a retrospective glance at the two powers, one of which annihilated the other on December 2, 1851, whereas from December 20, 1848, until the exit of the Constituent Assembly, they had lived in conjugal relations. We mean Louis Bonaparte, on the one hand, and the party of the coalesced royalists, the party of Order, of the big bourgeoisie, on the other. On acceding to the presidency, Bonaparte at once formed a ministry of the party of Order, at the head of which he placed Odilon Barrot, the old leader, *nota bene,** of the most liberal faction of the parliamentary bourgeoisie. M. Barrot had at last secured the ministerial portfolio, the spectre of which had haunted him since 1830, and what is more, the premiership in the ministry; but not, as he had imagined under Louis Philippe, as the most advanced leader of the parliamentary opposition, but with the task of putting a parliament to death, and as the confederate of all his arch-enemies, Jesuits and Legitimists. He brought the bride home at last, but only after she had been prostituted. Bonaparte seemed to efface himself completely. This party acted for him.

The very first meeting of the council of ministers resolved on the expedition to Rome, which, it was agreed, should be undertaken behind the back of the National Assembly and the means for which were to be wrested from it by false pretences. Thus they began by swindling the National Assembly and secretly conspiring with the absolutist powers abroad against the revolutionary Roman republic. In the same manner and with the same manoeuvres Bonaparte prepared his *coup* of December 2 against the royalist Legislative Assembly and its constitutional republic. Let us not forget that the same party which formed Bonaparte's ministry on December 20, 1848, formed the majority of the Legislative National Assembly on December 2, 1851.

In August the Constituent Assembly had decided to dissolve only after it had worked out and promulgated a whole series of organic laws that were to supplement the Constitution. On January 6, 1849, the party of Order had a deputy named Rateau move that the Assembly should let the organic laws go and rather decide on its *own dissolution.* Not only the ministry, with Odilon Barrot at its head, but

---

*Literally, note well (Latin); a request to pay heed.

all the royalist members of the National Assembly told it in bullying accents then that its dissolution was necessary for the restoration of credit, for the consolidation of order, for putting an end to the indefinite provisional arrangements and for establishing a definitive state of affairs; that it hampered the productivity of the new government and sought to prolong its existence merely out of malice; that the country was tired of it. Bonaparte took note of all this invective against the legislative power, learnt it by heart and proved to the parliamentary royalists, on December 2, 1851, that he had learnt from them. He reiterated their own catchwords against them.

The Barrot ministry and the party of Order went further. They caused *petitions to the National Assembly* to be made throughout France, in which this body was politely requested to deeamp. They thus led the unorganized popular masses into the fire of battle against the National Assembly, the constitutionally organized expression of the people. They taught Bonaparte to appeal against the parliamentary assemblies to the people. At length, on January 29, 1849, the day had come on which the Constituent Assembly was to decide concerning its own dissolution. The National Assembly found the building where its sessions were held occupied by the military; Changarnier, the general of the party of Order, in whose hands the supreme command of the National Guard and troops of the line had been united, held a great military review in Paris, as if a battle were impending, and the royalists in coalition threateningly declared to the Constituent Assembly that force would be employed if it should prove unwilling. It was willing, and only bargained for a very short extra term of life. What was January 29 but the *coup d'état* of December 2, 1851, only carried out by the royalists with Bonaparte against the republican National Assembly? The gentlemen did not observe, or did not wish to observe, that Bonaparte availed himself of January 29, 1849, to have a portion of the troops march past him in front of the Tuileries, and seized with avidity on just this first public summoning of the military power against the parliamentary power to foreshadow Caligula.* They, to be sure, saw only their Changarnier.

---

*Gaius Caesar Germanicus (A.D. 12–41), Roman emperor whose childhood nickname was Caligula (Latin for "Little Boot"); known for his ruthless cruelty, he was assassinated by members of his Praetorian guard.

A motive that particularly actuated the party of Order in forcibly cutting short the duration of the Constituent Assembly's life was the organic laws supplementing the Constitution, such as the education law, the law on religious worship, etc. To the royalists in coalition it was most important that they themselves should make these laws and not let them be made by the republicans, who had grown mistrustful. Among these organic laws, however, was also a law on the responsibility of the President of the republic. In 1851 the Legislative Assembly was occupied with the drafting of just such a law, when Bonaparte anticipated this *coup* with the *coup* of December 2. What would the royalists in coalition not have given in their parliamentary winter campaign of 1851 to have found the Responsibility Law ready to hand, and drawn up, at that, by a mistrustful, hostile, republican Assembly!

After the Constituent Assembly had itself shattered its last weapon on January 29, 1849, the Barrot ministry and the friends of order hounded it to death, left nothing undone that could humiliate it and wrested from the impotent, self-despairing Assembly laws that cost it the last remnant of respect in the eyes of the public. Bonaparte, occupied with his fixed Napoleonic idea, was brazen enough to exploit publicly this degradation of the parliamentary power. For when on May 8, 1849, the National Assembly passed a vote of censure of the ministry because of the occupation of Civitavecchia by Oudinot, and ordered it to bring back the Roman expedition to its alleged purpose,* Bonaparte published the same evening in the *Moniteur*† a letter to Oudinot, in which he congratulated him on his heroic exploits and, in contrast to the ink-slinging parliamentarians, already posed as the generous protector of the army. The royalists smiled at this. They regarded him simply as their dupe. Finally, when Marrast, the President of the Constituent Assembly, believed for a moment that the safety of the National Assembly was endangered and, relying on the Constitution, requisitioned a colonel and his regiment, the colonel declined, cited discipline in his support and referred Marrast to Changarnier, who scornfully refused him with the

---

*Contrary to its official mission, the French army had fought against the Roman Republic, not on behalf of it.
†Governmental journal.

remark that he did not like *baïonnettes intelligentes.* In November 1851, when the royalists in coalition wanted to begin the decisive struggle with Bonaparte, they sought to put through in their notorious *Quaestors' Bill,* the principle of the direct requisition of troops by the President of the National Assembly. One of their generals, Le Flô, had signed the bill. In vain did Changarnier vote for it and Thiers pay homage to the far-sighted wisdom of the former Constituent Assembly. The *War Minister, Saint-Arnaud,* answered him as Changarnier had answered Marrast—and to the acclamation of the *Montagne!**

Thus the *party of Order,* when it was not yet the National Assembly, when it was still only the ministry, had itself stigmatized the *parliamentary regime.* And it makes an outcry when December 2, 1851 banished this regime from France!

We wish it a happy journey.

---

*Name of the parliamentary representatives of the social-democratic party; see also pp. 93–95.

III

On May 28, 1849, the Legislative National Assembly met. On December 2, 1851, it was dispersed. This period covers the span of life of the *constitutional, or parliamentary, republic.*

In the first French Revolution the rule of the *Constitutionalists* is followed by the rule of the *Girondists* and the rule of the *Girondists* by the rule of the *Jacobins.** Each of these parties relies on the more progressive party for support. As soon as it has brought the revolution far enough to be unable to follow it further, still less to go ahead of it, it is thrust aside by the bolder ally that stands behind it and sent to the guillotine. The revolution thus moves along an ascending line.

It is the reverse with the Revolution of 1848. The proletarian party appears as an appendage of the petty-bourgeois-democratic party. It is betrayed and dropped by the latter on April 16, May 15, and in the June days. The democratic party, in its turn, leans on the shoulders of the bourgeois-republican party. The bourgeois republicans no sooner believe themselves well established than they shake off the troublesome comrade and support themselves on the shoulders of the party of Order. The party of Order hunches its shoulders, lets the bourgeois republicans tumble and throws itself on the shoulders of armed force. It fancies it is still sitting on its shoulders when, one fine morning, it perceives that the shoulders have transformed themselves into bayonets. Each party kicks from behind at that driving forward and in front leans over towards the party which presses backwards. No wonder that in this ridiculous posture it loses its balance and, having made the inevitable grimaces, collapses with curious capers. The revolution thus moves in a descending line. It finds itself in this state of retrogressive motion before the last February barricade has been cleared away and the first revolutionary authority constituted.

The period that we have before us comprises the most motley mixture of crying contradictions: constitutionalists who conspire

---

*Different political clubs and factions that successively dominated the French Revolution; the Jacobins, headed by Maximilien de Robespierre (1758–1794), were the most radical, the Constitutionalists the most moderate.

openly against the Constitution; revolutionists who are confessedly constitutional; a National Assembly that wants to be omnipotent and always remains parliamentary; a *Montagne* that finds its vocation in patience and counters its present defeats by prophesying future victories; royalists who form the *patres conscripti** of the republic and are forced by the situation to keep the hostile royal houses, to which they adhere, abroad, and the republic, which they hate, in France; an executive power that finds its strength in its very weakness and its respectability in the contempt that it calls forth; a republic that is nothing but the combined infamy of two monarchies, the Restoration and the July Monarchy, with an imperial label—alliances whose first proviso is separation; struggles whose first law is indecision; wild, inane agitation in the name of tranquillity, most solemn preaching of tranquillity in the name of revolution; passions without truth, truths without passion; heroes without heroic deeds, history without events; development, whose sole driving force seems to be the calendar, wearying with constant repetition of the same tensions and relaxations; antagonisms that periodically seem to work themselves up to a climax only to lose their sharpness and fall away without being able to resolve themselves; pretentiously paraded exertions and philistine terror at the danger of the world coming to an end, and at the same time the pettiest intrigues and court comedies played by the world redeemers, who in their *laisser aller*† remind us less of the Day of Judgment than of the times of the Fronde—the official collective genius of France brought to naught by the artful stupidity of a single individual; the collective will of the nation, as often as it speaks through universal suffrage, seeking its appropriate expression through the inveterate enemies of the interests of the masses, until, at length, it finds it in the self-will of a filibuster. If any section of history has been painted grey on grey, it is this. Men and events appear as inverted Schlemihls, as shadows that have lost their bodies. The revolution itself paralyzes its own bearers and endows only its adversaries with passionate forcefulness. When the "red spectre," continually conjured up and exorcised by the counter-revolutionaries, finally appears, it appears not with the

---

*Senators (Latin).
†Letting go (French).

Phrygian cap of anarchy on its head, but in the uniform of order, in *red breeches.*

We have seen that the ministry which Bonaparte installed on December 20, 1848, on his Ascension Day, was a ministry of the party of Order, of the Legitimist and Orleanist coalition. This Barrot-Falloux ministry had outlived the republican Constituent Assembly, whose term of life it had more or less violently cut short, and found itself still at the helm. Changarnier, the general of the allied royalists, continued to unite in his person the general command of the First Army Division and of the National Guard of Paris. Finally, the general elections had secured the party of Order a large majority in the National Assembly. Here the deputies and peers of Louis Philippe encountered a hallowed host of Legitimists, for whom many of the nation's ballots had become transformed into admission cards to the political stage. The Bonapartist representatives of the people were too sparse to be able to form an independent parliamentary party. They appeared merely as the *mauvaise queue** of the party of Order. Thus the party of Order was in possession of the governmental power, the army and the legislative body, in short, of the whole of the state power; it had been morally strengthened by the general elections, which made its rule appear as the will of the people, and by the simultaneous triumph of the counter-revolution on the whole continent of Europe.

Never did a party open its campaign with greater resources or under more favorable auspices.

The shipwrecked *pure republicans* found that they had melted down to a clique of about fifty men in the Legislative National Assembly, the African generals Cavaignac, Lamoricière and Bedeau at their head. The great opposition party, however, was formed by the *Montagne.* The *social-democratic* party had given itself this parliamentary baptismal name. It commanded more than two hundred of the seven hundred and fifty votes of the National Assembly and was consequently at least as powerful as any one of the three factions of the party of Order taken by itself. Its numerical inferiority compared with the entire royalist coalition seemed compensated by special circumstances. Not only did the elections in the Departments show

---

*Bad appendage.

that it had gained a considerable following among the rural population. It counted in its ranks almost all the deputies from Paris; the
army had made a confession of democratic faith by the election of
three non-commissioned officers, and the leader of the *Montagne,*
Ledru-Rollin, in contra-distinction to all the representatives of the
party of Order, had been raised to the parliamentary peerage by five
Departments, which had pooled their votes for him. In view of the
inevitable clashes of the royalists among themselves and of the
whole party of Order with Bonaparte, the *Montagne* thus seemed to
have all the elements of success before it on May 28, 1849. A fortnight later it had lost everything, honour included.

Before we pursue parliamentary history further, some remarks
are necessary to avoid common misconceptions regarding the whole
character of the epoch that lies before us. Looked at with the eyes of
democrats, the period of the Legislative National Assembly is concerned with what the period of the Constituent Assembly was concerned with: the simple struggle between republicans and royalists.
The movement itself, however, they sum up in the one shibboleth:*
"*reaction*"—night, in which all cats are grey† and which permits
them to reel off their night watchman's commonplaces. And, to be
sure, at first sight the party of Order, reveals a maze of different royalist factions, which not only intrigue against each other—each
seeking to elevate its own pretender to the throne and exclude the
pretender of the opposing faction—but also all unite in common
hatred of, and common onslaughts on, the "republic." In opposition
to this royalist conspiracy the *Montagne,* for its part, appears as the
representative of the "republic." The party of Order appears to be
perpetually engaged in a "reaction," directed against press, association and the like, neither more nor less than in Prussia, and which,
as in Prussia, is carried out in the form of brutal police intervention
by the bureaucracy, the *gendarmerie* and the law courts. The *"Montagne,"* for its part, is just as continually occupied in warding off

---

*Catchword or meaningless saying.
†Marx may be alluding to the German philosopher Georg Wilhelm Friedrich Hegel
(1770–1831), who used this expression to characterize empty abstraction—that is,
one that conceals particulars and differences. In the same way, Marx suggests that the
word "reaction" becomes a useless term because it is too abstract and thus disregards
important differences.

these attacks and thus defending the "eternal rights of man" as every so-called people's party has done, more or less, for a century and a half. If one looks at the situation and the parties more closely, however, this superficial appearance, which veils the *class struggle* and the peculiar physiognomy of this period, disappears.

Legitimists and Orleanists, as we have said, formed the two great factions of the party of Order. Was that which held these factions fast to their pretenders and kept them apart from one another nothing but lily and tricolour, House of Bourbon and House of Orleans, different shades of royalism, was it at all the confession of faith of royalism? Under the Bourbons, *big landed property* had governed, with its priests and lackeys; under the Orleans, high finance, large-scale industry, large-scale trade, that is, *capital*, with its retinue of lawyers, professors and smooth-tongued orators. The Legitimate Monarchy was merely the political expression of the hereditary rule of the lords of the soil, as the July Monarchy was only the political expression of the usurped rule of the bourgeois *parvenus.** What kept the two factions apart, therefore, was not any so-called principles, it was their material conditions of existence, two different kinds of property, it was the old contrast between town and country, the rivalry between capital and landed property. That at the same time old memories, personal enmities, fears and hopes, prejudices and illusions, sympathies and antipathies, convictions, articles of faith and principles bound them to one or the other royal house, who denies this? Upon the different forms of property, upon the social conditions of existence, rises an entire superstructure of distinct and peculiarly formed sentiments, illusions, modes of thought and views of life. The entire class creates and forms them out of its material foundations and out of the corresponding social relations. The single individual, who derives them through tradition and upbringing, may imagine that they form the real motives and the starting point of his activity. While Orleanists and Legitimists, while each faction sought to make itself and the other believe that it was loyalty to their two royal houses which separated them, facts later proved that it was rather their divided interests which forbade the uniting of the two royal houses. And as in private life one differentiates between what a man thinks and says of

---

*Newly rich persons.

himself and what he really is and does, so in historical struggles one must distinguish still more the phrases and fancies of parties from their real organism and their real interests, their conception of themselves, from their reality. Orleanists and Legitimists found themselves side by side in the republic, with equal claims. If each side wished to effect the *restoration* of its *own* royal house against the other, that merely signified that each of the *two great interests* into which the *bourgeoisie* is split—landed property and capital—sought to restore its own supremacy and the subordination of the other. We speak of two interests of the bourgeoisie, for large landed property, despite its feudal coquetry and pride of race, has been rendered thoroughly bourgeois by the development of modern society. Thus the Tories in England long imagined that they were enthusiastic about monarchy, the church and the beauties of the old English Constitution, until the day of danger wrung from them the confession that they are enthusiastic only about *ground rent.*

The royalists in coalition carried on their intrigues against one another in the press, in Ems,* in Claremont,† outside parliament. Behind the scenes they donned their old Orleanist and Legitimist liveries again and once more engaged in their old tourneys. But on the public stage, in their grand performances of state, as a great parliamentary party, they put off their respective royal houses with mere obeisances and adjourn the restoration of the monarchy *in infinitum.* They do their real business as the *party of Order*, that is, under a *social,* not under a *political* title; as representatives of the bourgeois world-order, not as knights of errant princesses; as the bourgeois class against other classes, not as royalists against the republicans. And as the party of Order they exercised more unrestricted and sterner domination over the other classes of society than ever previously under the Restoration or under the July Monarchy, a domination which, in general, was only possible under the form of the parliamentary republic, for only under this form could the two great divisions of the French bourgeoisie unite, and thus put

---

*Bad Ems, a German spa town where the Legitimists (see footnote on p. 82) met in 1849.

†After being dethroned by the February Revolution of 1848, Louis Philippe fled to Claremont, near London, where he died in 1850.

the rule of their class instead of the regime of a privileged faction of it on the order of the day. If, nevertheless, they, as the party of Order, also insulted the republic and expressed their repugnance to it, this happened not merely from royalist memories. Instinct taught them that the republic, true enough, makes their political rule complete, but at the same time undermines its social foundation, since they must now confront the subjugated classes and contend against them without mediation, without the concealment afforded by the crown, without being able to divert the national interest by their subordinate struggles among themselves and with the monarchy. It was a feeling of weakness that caused them to recoil from the pure conditions of their own class rule and to yearn for the former more incomplete, more undeveloped and precisely on that account less dangerous forms of this rule. On the other hand, every time the royalists in coalition come in conflict with the pretender that confronts them, with Bonaparte, every time they believe their parliamentary omnipotence endangered by the executive power, every time, therefore, that they must produce their political title to their rule, they come forward as *republicans* and not as *royalists*, from the Orleanist Thiers, who warns the National Assembly that the republic divides them least, to the Legitimist Berryer, who, on December 2, 1851, as a tribune swathed in a tricoloured sash, harangues the people assembled before the town hall of the tenth *arrondissement** in the name of the republic. To be sure, a mocking echo calls back to him: Henry V! Henry V!†

As against the coalesced bourgeoisie, a coalition between petty bourgeois and workers had been formed, the so-called *social-democratic* party. The petty bourgeois saw that they were badly rewarded after the June days of 1848, that their material interests were imperilled and that the democratic guarantees which were to ensure the effectuation of these interests were called in question by the counter-revolution. Accordingly, they came closer to the workers. On the other hand, their parliamentary representation, the *Montagne*, thrust aside during the dictatorship of the bourgeois republi-

---

*One of the twenty administrative districts within the city of Paris.
†Henri-Dieudonné d'Artois, count de Chambord (1820–1883), was the grandson of King Charles X and the pretender to the French throne supported by the Legitimists.

cans, had in the last half of the life of the Constituent Assembly reconquered its lost popularity through the struggle with Bonaparte
and the royalist ministers. It had concluded an alliance with the socialist leaders. In February 1849, banquets celebrated the reconciliation. A joint program was drafted, joint election committees were set
up and joint candidates put forward. From the social demands of the
proletariat the revolutionary point was broken off and a democratic
turn given to them; from the democratic claims of the petty bourgeoisie the purely political form was stripped off and their socialist
point thrust forward. Thus arose the *Social-Democracy*. The new
Montagne, the result of this combination, contained, apart from
some supernumeraries from the working class and some socialist
sectarians, the same elements as the old *Montagne*, only numerically
stronger. However, in the course of development, it had changed
with the class that it represented. The peculiar character of the
Social-Democracy is epitomized in the fact that democratic-republican
institutions are demanded as a means, not of doing away with two
extremes, capital and wage labour, but of weakening their antagonism and transforming it into harmony. However different the
means proposed for the attainment of this end may be, however
much it may be trimmed with more or less revolutionary notions,
the content remains the same. This content is the transformation of
society in a democratic way, but a transformation within the bounds
of the petty bourgeoisie. Only one must not form the narrow-
minded notion that the petty bourgeoisie, on principle, wishes to
enforce an egoistic class interest. Rather, it believes that the *special*
conditions of its emancipation are the *general* conditions within the
frame of which alone modern society can be saved and the class
struggle avoided. Just as little must one imagine that the democratic
representatives are indeed all shopkeepers or enthusiastic champi-
ons of shopkeepers. According to their education and their individual position they may be as far apart as heaven from earth. What
makes them representatives of the petty bourgeoisie is the fact that
in their minds they do not get beyond the limits which the latter do
not get beyond in life, that they are consequently driven, theoretically, to the same problems and solutions to which material interest
and social position drive the latter practically. This is, in general, the

relationship between the *political* and *literary representatives* of a class and the class they represent.

After the analysis given, it is obvious that if the *Montagne* continually contends with the party of Order for the republic and the so-called rights of man, neither the republic nor the rights of man are its final end, any more than an army which one wants to deprive of its weapons and which resists has taken the field in order to remain in possession of its own weapons.

Immediately, as soon as the National Assembly met, the party of Order provoked the *Montagne*. The bourgeoisie now felt the necessity of making an end of the democratic petty bourgeois, just as a year before it had realized the necessity of settling with the revolutionary proletariat. Only the situation of the adversary was different. The strength of the proletarian party lay in the streets, that of the petty bourgeois in the National Assembly itself. It was therefore a question of decoying them out of the National Assembly into the streets and causing them to smash their parliamentary power themselves, before time and circumstances could consolidate it. The *Montagne* rushed headlong into the trap.

The bombardment of Rome by the French troops was the bait that was thrown to it. It violated Article V of the Constitution which forbids the French republic to employ its military forces against the freedom of another people. In addition to this, Article 54 prohibited any declaration of war on the part of the executive power without the assent of the National Assembly, and by its resolution of May 8, the Constituent Assembly had disapproved of the Roman expedition. On these grounds Ledru-Rollin brought in a bill of impeachment against Bonaparte and his ministers on June 11, 1849. Exasperated by the wasp stings of Thiers, he actually let himself be carried away to the point of threatening that he would defend the Constitution by every means, even with arms in hand. The *Montagne* rose to a man and repeated this call to arms. On June 12, the National Assembly rejected the bill of impeachment, and the *Montagne* left the parliament. The events of June 13 are known: the proclamation issued by a section of the *Montagne*, declaring Bonaparte and his ministers "outside the Constitution"; the street procession of the democratic National Guards, who, unarmed as they were, dispersed on encountering the troops of Changarnier, etc., etc. A part of the *Montagne* fled abroad; another part was arraigned before the High Court at Bourges, and a parliamentary regulation subjected the remainder to the schoolmasterly surveillance of the President of the National Assembly. Paris was again declared in a state of siege and the democratic part of its National Guard dissolved. Thus the influence of the *Montagne* in parliament and the power of the petty bourgeois in Paris were broken.

Lyons, where June 13 had given the signal for a bloody insurrection of the workers, was, along with the five surrounding Departments, likewise declared in a state of siege, a condition that has continued up to the present moment.

The bulk of the *Montagne* had left its vanguard in the lurch, having refused to subscribe to its proclamation. The press had deserted, only two journals having dared to publish the *pronunciamento*.* The petty bourgeois betrayed their representatives, in that the National Guards either stayed away or, where they appeared, hindered the erection of barricades. The representatives had duped the petty bourgeois, in that the alleged allies from the army were nowhere to be seen. Finally, instead of gaining an accession of strength from it, the democratic party had infected the proletariat with its own weakness and, as is usual with the great deeds of democrats, the leaders had the satisfaction of being able to charge their "people" with desertion, and the people the satisfaction of being able to charge its leaders with humbugging it.

Seldom had an action been announced with more noise than the impending campaign of the *Montagne*, seldom had an event been trumpeted with greater certainty or longer in advance than the inevitable victory of the democracy. Most assuredly, the democrats believe in the trumpets before whose blasts the walls of Jericho fell down. And as often as they stand before the ramparts of despotism, they seek to imitate the miracle. If the *Montagne* wished to triumph in parliament, it should not have called to arms. If it called to arms in parliament, it should not have acted in parliamentary fashion in the streets. If the peaceful demonstration was meant seriously, then it was folly not to foresee that it would be given a war-like reception.

---

*Public proclamation (Italian).

If a real struggle was intended, then it was a queer idea to lay down the weapons with which it would have to be waged. But the revolutionary threats of the petty bourgeois and their democratic representatives are mere attempts to intimidate the antagonist. And when they have run into a blind alley, when they have sufficiently compromised themselves to make it necessary to give effect to their threats, then this is done in an ambiguous fashion that avoids nothing so much as the means to the end and tries to find excuses for succumbing. The blaring overture that announced the contest dies away in a pusillanimous snarl as soon as the struggle has to begin, the actors cease to take themselves *au sérieux*, and the action collapses completely, like a pricked bubble.

No party exaggerates its means more than the democratic, none deludes itself more light-mindedly over the situation. Since a section of the army had voted for it, the *Montagne* was now convinced that the army would revolt for it. And on what occasion? On an occasion which, from the standpoint of the troops, had no other meaning than that the revolutionists took the side of the Roman soldiers against the French soldiers. On the other hand, the recollections of June 1848 were still too fresh to allow of anything but a profound aversion on the part of the proletariat towards the National Guard and a thorough-going mistrust of the democratic chiefs on the part of the chiefs of the secret societies. To iron out these differences, it was necessary for great, common interests to be at stake. The violation of an abstract paragraph of the Constitution could not provide these interests. Had not the Constitution been repeatedly violated, according to the assurance of the democrats themselves? Had not the most popular journals branded it as counter-revolutionary botch-work? But the democrat, because he represents the petty bourgeoisie, that is, a *transition class*, in which the interests of two classes are simultaneously mutually blunted, imagines himself elevated above class antagonism generally. The democrats concede that a privileged class confronts them, but they, along with all the rest of the nation, form the *people*. What they represent is the *people's rights*; what interests them is the *people's interests*. Accordingly, when a struggle is impending, they do not need to examine the interests and positions of the different classes. They do not need to weigh their own resources too critically. They have merely to give the signal and the *people*, with all its inexhaustible resources, will fall upon the *oppressors*. Now, if in the performance their interests prove to be uninteresting and their potency impotence, then either the fault lies with pernicious sophists, who split the *indivisible people* into different hostile camps, or the army was too brutalized and blinded to comprehend that the pure aims of democracy are the best thing for it itself, or the whole thing has been wrecked by a detail in its execution, or else an unforeseen accident has this time spoilt the game. In any case, the democrat comes out of the most disgraceful defeat just as immaculate as he was innocent when he went into it, with the newly-won conviction that he is bound to win, not that he himself and his party have to give up the old standpoint, but, on the contrary, that conditions have to ripen to suit him.

Accordingly, one must not imagine the *Montagne*, decimated and broken though it was, and humiliated by the new parliamentary regulation, as being particularly miserable. If June 13 had removed its chiefs, it made room, on the other hand, for men of lesser calibre, whom this new position flattered. If their impotence in parliament could no longer be doubted, they were entitled now to confine their actions to outbursts of moral indignation and blustering declamation. If the party of Order affected to see embodied in them, as the last official representatives of the revolution, all the terrors of anarchy, they could in reality be all the more insipid and modest. They consoled themselves, however, for June 13 with the profound utterance: But if they dare to attack universal suffrage, well then—then we'll show them what we are made of! *Nous verrons!**

So far as the *Montagnards* who fled abroad are concerned, it is sufficient to remark here that Ledru-Rollin, because in barely a fortnight he had succeeded in ruining irretrievably the powerful party at whose head he stood, now found himself called upon to form a French government *in partibus*;† that to the extent that the level of the revolution sank and the official bigwigs of official France became more dwarf-like, his figure in the distance, removed from the scene

---

*We will see! (French).

†Marx refers to a practice in which the Catholic Church appointed bishops to non-Christian countries where the Church had no influence. These useless and powerless bishops were called bishops *in partibus infidelium*—bishops whose dioceses were located "in non-Christian countries."

of action, seemed to grow in stature; that he could figure as the republican pretender for 1852, and that he issued periodical circulars to the Wallachians and other peoples, in which the despots of the Continent are threatened with the deeds of himself and his confederates. Was Proudhon altogether wrong when he cried to these gentlemen: "*Vous n'êtes que des blagueurs*"?*

On June 13, the party of Order had not only broken the *Montagne*, it had effected the *subordination of the Constitution to the majority decisions of the National Assembly*. And it understood the republic thus: that the bourgeoisie rules here in parliamentary forms, without, as in a monarchy, encountering any barrier such as the veto power of the executive or the right to dissolve parliament. This was a *parliamentary republic*, as Thiers termed it. But whereas on June 13 the bourgeoisie secured its omnipotence within the house of parliament, did it not afflict parliament itself, as against the executive authority and the people, with incurable weakness by expelling its most popular part? By surrendering numerous deputies without further ado on the demand of the courts, it abolished its own parliamentary immunity. The humiliating regulations to which it subjected the *Montagne* exalted the President of the republic in the same measure as it degraded the individual representatives of the people. By branding an insurrection for the protection of the constitutional charter an anarchic act aiming at the subversion of society, it precluded the possibility of its appealing to insurrection should the executive authority violate the Constitution in relation to it. And by the irony of history, the general who on Bonaparte's instructions bombarded Rome and thus provided the immediate occasion for the constitutional revolt of June 13, that *Oudinot* had to be the man offered by the party of Order imploringly and unavailingly to the people as general on behalf of the Constitution against Bonaparte on December 2, 1851. Another hero of June 13, *Vieyra*, who was lauded from the tribune of the National Assembly for the brutalities that he had committed in the democratic newspaper offices at the head of a gang of National Guards belonging to high finance circles—this same Vieyra had been initiated into Bonaparte's conspiracy and he essentially contributed to depriving the National

---

*Jokers, pranksters (French).

Assembly in the hour of its death of any protection by the National Guard.

June 13 had still another meaning. The *Montagne* had wanted to force the impeachment of Bonaparte. Its defeat was therefore a direct victory for Bonaparte, his personal triumph over his democratic enemies. The party of Order gained the victory; Bonaparte had only to cash in on it. He did so. On June 14 a proclamation could be read on the walls of Paris in which the President, reluctantly, against his will, as it were, compelled by the sheer force of events, comes forth from his cloistered seclusion and, posing as misunderstood virtue, complains of the calumnies of his opponents and, while he seems to identify his person with the cause of order, rather identifies the cause of order with his person. Moreover, the National Assembly had, it is true, subsequently approved the expedition against Rome, but Bonaparte had taken the initiative in the matter. After having reinstalled the High Priest Samuel in the Vatican, he could hope to enter the Tuileries as King David.* He had won the priests over to his side.

The revolt of June 13 was confined, as we have seen, to a peaceful street procession. No war laurels were, therefore, to be won against it. Nevertheless, at a time as poor as this in heroes and events, the party of Order transformed this bloodless battle into a second Austerlitz. Platform and press praised the army as the power of order, in contrast to the popular masses, representing the impotence of anarchy, and extolled Changarnier as the "bulwark of society," a deception in which he himself finally came to believe. Surreptitiously, however, the corps that seemed doubtful were transferred from Paris, the regiments which had shown at the elections the most democratical sentiments were banished from France to Algiers, the turbulent spirits among the troops were relegated to penal detachments, and finally the isolation of the press from the barracks and of the barracks from bourgeois society was systematically carried out.

Here we have reached the decisive turning point in the history of the French National Guard. In 1830 it was decisive in the overthrow of the Restoration. Under Louis Philippe every rebellion miscarried in which the National Guard stood on the side of the troops. When in the February days of 1848 it evinced a passive attitude towards the

---

*In the Bible, the prophet Samuel anoints David king of Israel; see 1 Samuel 16:1–13.

insurrection and an equivocal one towards Louis Philippe, he gave himself up for lost and actually was lost. Thus the conviction took root that the revolution could not be victorious *without* the National Guard, nor the army *against* it. This was the superstition of the army in regard to civilian omnipotence. The June days of 1848, when the entire National Guard, with the troops of the line, put down the insurrection, had strengthened the superstition. After Bonaparte's assumption of office, the position of the National Guard was to some extent weakened by the unconstitutional union, in the person of Changarnier, of the command of its forces with the command of the First Army Division.

Just as the command of the National Guard appeared here as an attribute of the military commander-in-chief, so the National Guard itself appeared as only an appendage of the troops of the line. Finally, on June 13 its power was broken, and not only by its partial disbandment, which from this time on was periodically repeated all over France, until mere fragments of it were left behind. The demonstration of June 13 was, above all, a demonstration of the democratic National Guards. They had not, to be sure, borne their arms, but worn their uniforms against the army; precisely in this uniform, however, lay the talisman. The army convinced itself that this uniform was a piece of woollen cloth like any other. The spell was broken. In the June days of 1848, bourgeoisie and petty bourgeoisie had united as the National Guard with the army against the proletariat; on June 13, 1849. the bourgeoisie let the petty-bourgeois National Guard be dispersed by the army; on December 2, 1851, the National Guard of the bourgeoisie itself had vanished, and Bonaparte merely registered this fact when he subsequently signed the decree for its disbandment. Thus the bourgeoisie had itself smashed its last weapon against the army, the moment the petty bourgeoisie no longer stood behind it as a vassal, but before it as a rebel, it had to smash it as in general it was bound to destroy all its means of defence against absolutism with its own hand as soon as it had itself become absolute.

Meanwhile, the party of Order celebrated the reconquest of a power that seemed lost in 1848 only to be found again, freed from its restraints, in 1849, celebrated by means of invectives against the republic and the Constitution, of curses on all future, present and past revolutions, including that which its own leaders had made, and in laws by which the press was muzzled, association destroyed and the state of siege regulated as an organic institution. The National Assembly then adjourned from the middle of August to the middle of October, after having appointed a permanent commission for the period of its absence. During this recess the Legitimists intrigued with Ems, the Orleanists—with Claremont, Bonaparte—by means of princely tours, and the Departmental Councils—in deliberations on a revision of the Constitution: incidents which regularly recur in the periodic recesses of the National Assembly and which I propose to discuss only when they become events. Here it may merely be remarked, in addition, that it was impolitic for the National Assembly to disappear for considerable intervals from the stage and leave only a single, albeit a sorry, figure to be seen at the head of the republic, that of Louis Bonaparte, while to the scandal of the public the party of Order fell asunder into its royalist component parts and followed its conflicting desires for Restoration. As often as the confused noise of *parliament* grew silent during these recesses and its body dissolved in the nation, it became unmistakably clear that only one thing was still wanting to complete the true form of this republic: to make the *former's* recess permanent and replace the *latter's* inscription: Liberté, Égalité, Fraternité by the unambiguous words: Infantry, Cavalry, Artillery!

IV

IN THE MIDDLE OF October 1849, the National Assembly met once more. On November 1, Bonaparte surprised it with a message in which he announced the dismissal of the Barrot-Falloux ministry and the formation of a new ministry. No one has ever sacked lackeys with less ceremony than Bonaparte his ministers. The kicks that were intended for the National Assembly were given in the meantime to Barrot and Co.

The Barrot ministry, as we have seen, had been composed of Legitimists and Orleanists, a ministry of the party of Order. Bonaparte had needed it to dissolve the republican Constituent Assembly, to bring about the expedition against Rome and to break the democratic party. Behind this ministry he had seemingly effaced himself, surrendered governmental power into the hands of the party of Order and donned the modest character mask that the responsible editor of a newspaper wore under Louis Philippe, the mask of the *homme de paille.** He now threw off a mask which was no longer the light veil behind which he could hide his physiognomy, but an iron mask which prevented him from displaying a physiognomy of his own. He had appointed the Barrot ministry in order to blast the republican National Assembly in the name of the party of Order; he dismissed it in order to declare his own name independent of the National Assembly of the party of Order.

Plausible pretexts for this dismissal were not lacking. The Barrot ministry neglected even the decencies that would have let the President of the republic appear as a power side by side with the National Assembly. During the recess of the National Assembly Bonaparte published a letter to Edgar Ney in which he seemed to disapprove of the illiberal attitude of the Pope, just as in opposition to the Constituent Assembly he had published a letter in which he commended Oudinot for the attack on the Roman republic. When the National Assembly now voted the budget for the Roman expedition, Victor

---

*Straw man (French).

Hugo, out of alleged liberalism, brought up this letter for discussion. The party of Order with scornfully incredulous outcries stifled the idea that Bonaparte's ideas could have any political importance. Not one of the ministers took up the gauntlet for him. On another occasion Barrot, with his well-known hollow rhetoric, let fall from the platform words of indignation concerning the "abominable intrigues" that, according to his assertion, went on in the immediate entourage of the President. Finally, while the ministry obtained from the National Assembly a widow's pension for the Duchess of Orleans it rejected any proposal to increase the Civil List of the President. And in Bonaparte the imperial pretender was so intimately bound up with the adventurer down on his luck that the one great idea, that he was called to restore the empire, was always supplemented by the other, that it was the mission of the French people to pay his debts.

The Barrot-Falloux ministry was the first and last *parliamentary ministry* that Bonaparte brought into being. Its dismissal forms, accordingly, a decisive turning-point. With it the party of Order lost, never to reconquer it, an indispensable post for the maintenance of the parliamentary regime, the lever of executive power. It is immediately obvious that in a country like France, where the executive power commands an army of officials numbering more than half a million individuals and therefore constantly maintains an immense mass of interests and livelihoods in the most absolute dependence; where the state enmeshes, controls, regulates, superintends and tutors civil society from its most comprehensive manifestations of life down to its most insignificant stirrings, from its most general modes of being to the private existence of individuals; where through the most extraordinary centralization this parasitic body acquires a ubiquity, an omniscience, a capacity for accelerated mobility and an elasticity which finds a counterpart only in the helpless dependence, in the loose shapelessness of the actual body politic—it is obvious that in such a country the National Assembly forfeits all real influence when it loses command of the ministerial posts, if it does not at the same time simplify the administration of the state, reduce the army of officials as far as possible and, finally, let civil society and public opinion create organs of their own, independent of the governmental power. But it is precisely with the maintenance of that extensive state machine in its numerous ramifications that the *material interests* of the French bourgeoisie are interwoven in the closest fashion. Here it finds posts for its surplus population and makes up in the form of state salaries for what it cannot pocket in the form of profit, interest, rents and honorariums. On the other hand, its *political interests* compelled it to increase daily the repressive measures and therefore the resources and the personnel of the state power, while at the same time it had to wage an uninterrupted war against public opinion and mistrustfully mutilate, cripple, the independent organs of the social movement, where it did not succeed in amputating them entirely. Thus the French bourgeoisie was compelled by its class position to annihilate, on the one hand, the vital conditions of all parliamentary power, and therefore, likewise, of its own, and to render irresistible, on the other hand, the executive power hostile to it.

The new ministry was called the d'Hautpoul ministry. Not in the sense that General d'Hautpoul had received the rank of Prime Minister. Rather, simultaneously with Barrot's dismissal, Bonaparte abolished this dignity, which, true enough, condemned the President of the republic to the status of the legal nonentity of a constitutional monarch, but of a constitutional monarch without throne or crown, without scepter or sword, without irresponsibility, without imprescriptible possession of the highest state dignity, and, worst of all, without a Civil List. The d'Hautpoul ministry contained only one man of parliamentary standing, the moneylender *Fould*, one of the most notorious of the high financiers. To his lot fell the ministry of finance. Look up the quotations on the Paris *bourse** and you will find that from November 1, 1849, onwards the French *fonds* rise and fall with the rise and fall of Bonapartist stocks. While Bonaparte had thus found his ally in the *bourse*, he at the same time took possession of the police by appointing Carlier Police Prefect of Paris.

Only in the course of development, however, could the consequences of the change of ministers come to light. To begin with, Bonaparte had taken a step forward only to be driven backward all the more conspicuously. His brusque message was followed by the most servile declaration of allegiance to the National Assembly. As often as the ministers dared to make a diffident attempt to introduce his personal fads as legislative proposals, they themselves seemed to

---

*Bourse: stock exchange; *fonds*: government securities (French).

carry out, against their will only and compelled by their position, comical commissions of whose fruitlessness they were persuaded in advance. As often as Bonaparte blurted out his intentions behind the ministers' backs and played with his "*idées napoléoniennes*,"* his own ministers disavowed him from the tribune of the National Assembly. His usurpatory longings seemed to make themselves heard only in order that the malicious laughter of his opponents might not be muted. He behaved like an unrecognized genius, whom all the world takes for a simpleton. Never did he enjoy the contempt of all classes in fuller measure than during this period. Never did the bourgeoisie rule more absolutely, never did it display more ostentatiously the insignia of domination.

I have not here to write the history of its legislative activity, which is summarized during this period in two laws: in the law re-establishing the *wine tax* and the *education law* abolishing unbelief. If wine drinking was made harder for the French, they were presented all the more plentifully with the water of true life. If in the law on the wine tax the bourgeoisie declared the old, hateful French tax system to be inviolable, it sought through the education law to ensure among the masses the old state of mind that put up with the tax system. One is astonished to see the Orleanists, the liberal bourgeois, these old apostles of Voltairianism and eclectic philosophy, entrust to their hereditary enemies, the Jesuits, the superintendence of the French mind. However, in regard to the pretenders to the throne, Orleanists and Legitimists could part company, they understood that to secure their united rule necessitated the uniting of the means of repression of two epochs, that the means of subjugation of the July Monarchy had to be supplemented and strengthened by the means of subjugation of the Restoration.

The peasants, disappointed in all their hopes, crushed more than ever by the low level of grain prices on the one hand, and by the growing burden of taxes and mortgage debts on the other, began to bestir themselves in the Departments. They were answered by a drive against the schoolmasters, who were made subject to the clergy, by a drive against the *maires*,† who were made subject to the

---

*Napoleonic ideas (French).
†Mayors (French).

prefects, and by a system of espionage, to which all were made subject. In Paris and the large towns reaction itself has the physiognomy of its epoch and challenges more than it strikes down. In the countryside it becomes dull, coarse, petty, tiresome and vexatious, in a word, the *gendarme*. One comprehends how three years of the regime of the *gendarme*,* consecrated by the regime of the priest, were bound to demoralize immature masses.

Whatever amount of passion and declamation might be employed by the party of Order against the minority from the tribune of the National Assembly, its speech remained as monosyllabic as that of the Christians, whose words were to be: Yea, yea; nay, nay! As monosyllabic on the platform as in the press. Flat as a riddle whose answer is known in advance. Whether it was a question of the right of petition or the tax on wine, freedom of the press or free trade, the clubs or the municipal charter, protection of personal liberty or regulation of the state budget, the watchword constantly recurs, the theme remains always the same, the verdict is ever ready and invariably reads: "*Socialism!*" Even bourgeois liberalism is declared *socialistic*, bourgeois enlightenment socialistic, bourgeois financial reform socialistic. It was socialistic to build a railway, where a canal already existed, and it was socialistic to defend oneself with a cane when one was attacked with a rapier.

This was not merely a figure of speech, fashion or party tactics. The bourgeoisie had a true insight into the fact that all the weapons which it had forged against feudalism turned their points against itself, that all the means of education which it had produced rebelled against its own civilization, that all the gods which it had created had fallen away from it. It understood that all the so-called bourgeois liberties and organs of progress attacked and menaced its *class rule* at its social foundation and its political summit simultaneously, and had therefore become "*socialistic.*" In this menace and this attack it rightly discerned the secret of Socialism, whose import and tendency it judges more correctly than so-called Socialism knows how to judge itself; the latter can, accordingly, not comprehend why the bourgeoisie callously hardens its heart against it, whether it sentimentally bewails the sufferings of mankind, or in Christian spirit

---

*Policeman (French).

prophesies the millennium and universal brotherly love, or in humanistic style twaddles about mind, education and freedom, or in doctrinaire fashion excogitates a system for the conciliation and welfare of all classes. What the bourgeoisie did not grasp, however, was the logical conclusion that its *own parliamentary regime*, that its *political rule* in general, was now also bound to meet with the general verdict of condemnation as being *socialistic*. As long as the rule of the bourgeois class had not been organized completely, as long as it had not acquired its pure political expression, the antagonism of the other classes, likewise, could not appear in its pure form, and where it did appear could not take the dangerous turn that transforms every struggle against the state power into a struggle against capital. If in every stirring of life in society it saw "tranquillity" imperilled, how could it want to maintain at the head of society a *regime of unrest*, its own regime, the *parliamentary regime*, this regime that, according to the expression of one of its spokesmen, lives in struggle and by struggle? The parliamentary regime lives by discussion; how shall it forbid discussion? Every interest, every social institution, is here transformed into general ideas, debated as ideas; how shall any interest, any institution, sustain itself above thought and impose itself as an article of faith? The struggle of the orators on the platform evokes the struggle of the scribblers of the press; the debating club in parliament is necessarily supplemented by debating clubs in the salons and the pothouses; the representatives, who constantly appeal to public opinion, give public opinion the right to speak its real mind in petitions. The parliamentary regime leaves everything to the decision of majorities; how shall the great majorities outside parliament not want to decide? When you play the fiddle at the top of the state, what else is to be expected but that those down below dance?

Thus, by now stigmatizing as "*socialistic*" what it had previously extolled as "*liberal*," the bourgeoisie confesses that its own interests dictate that it should be delivered from the danger of its *own rule*; that, in order to restore tranquillity in the country, its bourgeois parliament must, first of all, be given its quietus; that in order to preserve its social power intact, its political power must be broken; that the individual bourgeois can continue to exploit the other classes and to enjoy undisturbed property, family, religion and order only on condition that their class be condemned along with the other classes to like political nullity; that in order to save its purse, it must forfeit the crown, and the sword that is to safeguard it must at the same time be hung over its own head as a sword of Damocles.

In the domain of the interests of the general citizenry, the National Assembly showed itself so unproductive that, for example, the discussions on the Paris-Avignon railway, which began in the winter of 1850, were still not ripe for conclusion on December 2, 1851. Where it did not repress or pursue a reactionary course it was stricken with incurable barrenness.

While Bonaparte's ministry partly took the initiative in framing laws in the spirit of the party of Order, and partly even outdid that party's harshness in their execution and administration, he, on the other hand, by childishly silly proposals sought to win popularity, to bring out his opposition to the National Assembly, and to hint at a secret reserve that was only temporarily prevented by conditions from making its hidden treasures available to the French people. Such was the proposal to decree an increase in pay of four sous a day to the non-commissioned officers. Such was the proposal of an honour system loan bank for the workers. Money as a gift and money as a loan, it was with prospects such as these that he hoped to allure the masses. Donations and loans—the financial science of the *lumpenproletariat*, whether of high degree or low, is restricted to this. Such were the only springs which Bonaparte knew how to set in action. Never has a pretender speculated more stupidly on the stupidity of the masses.

The National Assembly flared up repeatedly over these unmistakable attempts to gain popularity at its expense, over the growing danger that this adventurer, whom his debts spurred on and no established reputation held back, would venture a desperate *coup*. The discord between the party of Order and the President had taken on a threatening character when an unexpected event threw him back repentant into its arms. We mean the *by-elections of March 10, 1850.* These elections were held for the purpose of filling the representatives' seats that after June 13 had been rendered vacant by imprisonment or exile. Paris elected only social-democratic candidates. It even concentrated most of the votes on an insurgent of June 1848, on Deflotte. Thus did the Parisian petty bourgeoisie, in alliance with the proletariat, revenge itself for its defeat on June 13, 1849. It seemed to have disappeared from the battlefield at the moment of danger only to reappear there on a more propitious occasion with more numerous fighting forces and with a bolder battle cry. One circumstance seemed to heighten the peril of this election victory. The army voted in Paris for the June insurgent against La Hitte, a minister of Bonaparte's, and in the Departments largely for the *Montagnards*, who here, too, though indeed not so decisively as in Paris, maintained the ascendancy over their adversaries.

Bonaparte saw himself suddenly confronted with revolution once more. As on January 29, 1849, as on June 13, 1849, so on March 10, 1850, he disappeared behind the party of Order. He made obeisance, he pusillanimously begged pardon, he offered to appoint any ministry it pleased at the behest of the parliamentary majority, he even implored the Orleanist and Legitimist party leaders, the Thiers, the Berryers, the Broglies, the Molés, in brief, the so-called burgraves,* to take the helm of state themselves. The party of Order proved unable to take advantage of this opportunity that would never return. Instead of boldly possessing itself of the power offered, it did not even compel Bonaparte to reinstate the ministry dismissed on November 1; it contented itself with humiliating him by its forgiveness and adjoining M. *Baroche* to the d'Hautpoul ministry. As public prosecutor this Baroche had stormed and raged before the High Court at Bourges, the first time against the revolutionists of May 15, the second time against the democrats of June 13, both times because of an attempt on the life of the National Assembly. None of Bonaparte's ministers subsequently contributed more to the degradation of the National Assembly, and after December 2, 1851, we meet him once more as the comfortably installed and highly paid Vice-President of the Senate. He had spat in the revolutionists' soup in order that Bonaparte might eat it up.

The social-democratic party, for its part, seemed only to try to find pretexts for putting its own victory once again in doubt and for blunting its point. Vidal, one of the newly elected representatives of Paris, had been elected simultaneously in Strasbourg. He was in-

---

*Name given to the representatives of the conservative Party of Order, a coalition of the Legitimists and the Orleanists (see footnotes on p. 82).

duced to decline the election for Paris and accept it for Strasbourg. And so, instead of making its victory at the polls conclusive and thereby compelling the party of Order at once to contest it in parliament, instead of thus forcing the adversary to fight at the moment of popular enthusiasm and favourable mood in the army, the democratic party wearied Paris during the months of March and April with a new election campaign, let the aroused popular passions wear themselves out in this repeated provisional election game, let the revolutionary energy satiate itself with constitutional successes, dissipate itself in petty intrigues, hollow declamations and sham movements, let the bourgeoisie rally and make its preparations, and, lastly, weakened the significance of the March elections by a sentimental commentary in the April by-election, the election of Eugène Sue. In a word, it made an April Fool of March 10.

The parliamentary majority understood the weakness of its antagonist. Its seventeen burgraves—for Bonaparte had left to it the direction of and responsibility for the attack—drew up a new electoral law, the introduction of which was entrusted to M. Faucher, who solicited this honour for himself. On May 8 he introduced the law by which universal suffrage was to be abolished, a residence of three years in the locality of the election to be imposed as a condition on the electors and, finally, the proof of this residence made dependent in the case of workers on a certificate from their employers.

Just as the democrats had, in revolutionary fashion, agitated the minds and raged during the constitutional election contest, so now, when it was requisite to prove the serious nature of that victory arms in hand, did they in constitutional fashion preach order, majestic calm (*calme majestueux*), lawful action, that is to say, blind subjection to the will of the counter-revolution, which imposed itself as the law. During the debate the Mountain put the party of Order to shame by asserting, against the latter's revolutionary passionateness, the dispassionate attitude of the philistine who keeps within the law, and by felling that party to earth with the fearful reproach that it proceeded in a revolutionary manner. Even the newly elected deputies were at pains to prove by their decorous and discreet action what a misconception it was to decry them as anarchists and construe their election as a victory for revolution. On May 31, the new electoral law went through. The *Montagne* contented itself with smuggling a protest into the pocket of the President. The electoral law was followed by a new press law, by which the revolutionary newspaper press was entirely suppressed. It had deserved its fate. The *National* and *La Presse*, two bourgeois organs, were left behind after this deluge as the most advanced outposts of the revolution.

We have seen how during March and April the democratic leaders had done everything to embroil the people of Paris in a sham fight, how after May 8 they did everything to restrain them from a real fight. In addition to this, we must not forget that the year 1850 was one of the most splendid years of industrial and commercial prosperity, and the Paris proletariat was therefore fully employed. But the election law of May 31, 1850, excluded it from any participation in political power. It cut it off from the very arena of the struggle. It threw the workers back into the position of pariahs which they had occupied before the February Revolution. By letting themselves be led by the democrats in face of such an event and forgetting the revolutionary interests of their class for momentary ease and comfort, they renounced the honour of being a conquering power, surrendered to their fate, proved that the defeat of June 1848 had put them out of the fight for years and that the historical process would for the present again have to go on *over* their heads. So far as the petty-bourgeois democracy is concerned, which on June 13 had cried: "But if once universal suffrage is attacked, then we'll show them!", it now consoled itself with the contention that the counter-revolutionary blow which had struck it was no blow and the law of May 31 no law. On the second Sunday in May 1852, every French-man would appear at the polling place with ballot in one hand and sword in the other. With this prophecy it rested content. Lastly, the army was disciplined by its superior officers for the elections of March and April 1850, just as it had been disciplined for those of May 28, 1849. This time, however, it said decidedly: "The revolution shall not dupe us a third time."

The law of May 31, 1850, was the *coup d'état* of the bourgeoisie. All its conquests over the revolution hitherto had only a provisional character. They were endangered as soon as the existing National Assembly retired from the stage. They depended on the hazards of a new general election, and the history of elections since 1848 irrefutably proved that the bourgeoisie's moral sway over the mass of the people was lost in the same measure as its actual domination developed. On March 10, universal suffrage declared itself directly against the domination of the bourgeoisie; the bourgeoisie answered by outlawing universal suffrage. The law of May 31 was, therefore, one of the necessities of the class struggle. On the other hand, the Constitution required a minimum of two million votes to make an election of the President of the republic valid. If none of the candidates for the presidency received this minimum, the National Assembly was to choose the President from among the three candidates to whom the largest number of votes would fall. At the time when the Constituent Assembly made this law, ten million electors were registered on the rolls of voters. In its view, therefore, a fifth of the people entitled to vote was sufficient to make the presidential election valid. The law of May 31 struck at least three million votes off the electoral rolls, reduced the number of people entitled to vote to seven million and, nevertheless, retained the legal minimum of two million for the presidential election. It therefore raised the legal minimum from a fifth to nearly a third of the effective votes, that is, it did everything to smuggle the election of the President out of the hands of the people and into the hands of the National Assembly. Thus through the electoral law of May 31 the party of Order seemed to have made its rule doubly secure, by surrendering the election of the National Assembly and that of the President of the republic to the stationary section of society.

V

As soon as the revolutionary crisis had been weathered and universal suffrage abolished, the struggle between the National Assembly and Bonaparte broke out again.

The Constitution had fixed Bonaparte's salary at 600,000 francs. Barely six months after his installation he succeeded in increasing this sum to twice as much, for Odilon Barrot wrung from the Constituent National Assembly an extra allowance of 600,000 francs a year for so-called representation moneys. After June 13, Bonaparte had caused similar requests to be voiced, this time without eliciting response from Barrot. Now, after May 31, he at once availed himself of the favourable moment and caused his ministers to propose a Civil List of three millions in the National Assembly. A long life of adventurous vagabondage had endowed him with the most developed antennae for feeling out the weak moments when he might squeeze money from his bourgeois. He practised regular *chantage*.* The National Assembly had violated the sovereignty of the people with his assistance and his cognizance. He threatened to denounce its crime to the tribunal of the people unless it loosened its purse strings and purchased his silence with three million a year. It had robbed three million Frenchmen of their franchise. He demanded, for every Frenchman out of circulation, a franc in circulation, precisely three million francs. He, the elect of six millions, claimed damages for the votes out of which he said he had retrospectively been cheated. The Commission of the National Assembly refused the importunate one. The Bonapartist press threatened. Could the National Assembly break with the President of the republic at a moment when in principle it had definitely broken with the mass of the nation? It rejected the annual Civil List, it is true, but it granted, for this once, an extra allowance of two million one hundred and sixty thousand francs. It thus rendered itself guilty of the double weakness of granting the money and of showing at the same time by its vexation that it granted it unwillingly. We shall see later for

---

*Extortion (French).

114

what purpose Bonaparte needed the money. After this vexatious aftermath, which followed on the heels of the abolition of universal suffrage and in which Bonaparte exchanged his humble attitude during the crisis of March and April for challenging impudence to the usurpatory parliament, the National Assembly adjourned for three months, from August 11 to November 11. In its place it left behind a Permanent Commission of twenty-eight members, which contained no Bonapartists, but did contain some moderate republicans. The Permanent Commission of 1849 had included only Order men and Bonapartists. But at that time the party of Order declared itself in permanence against the revolution. This time the parliamentary republic declared itself in permanence against the President. After the law of May 31, this was the only rival that still confronted the party of Order.

When the National Assembly met once more in November 1850, it seemed that, instead of the petty skirmishes it had hitherto had with the President, a great and ruthless struggle, a life-and-death struggle between the two powers, had become inevitable.

As in 1849 so during this year's parliamentary recess, the party of Order had broken up into its separate factions, each occupied with its own Restoration intrigues, which had obtained fresh nutriment through the death of Louis Philippe. The Legitimist king, Henry V, had even nominated a formal ministry which resided in Paris and in which members of the Permanent Commission held seats. Bonaparte, in his turn, was therefore entitled to make tours of the French Departments, and according to the disposition of the town that he favoured with his presence, now more or less covertly, now more or less overtly, to divulge his own restoration plans and canvass votes for himself. On these processions, which the great official *Moniteur* and the little private *Moniteurs* of Bonaparte naturally had to celebrate as triumphal processions, he was constantly accompanied by persons affiliated with the *Society of December 10*. This society dates from the year 1849. On the pretext of founding a benevolent society, the *lumpenproletariat* of Paris had been organized into secret sections, each section being led by Bonapartist agents, with a Bonapartist general at the head of the whole. Alongside decayed *roués**

Roués: debauched people (French); *mountebanks*: charlatans; *lazzaroni*: tramps (Italian); *maquereaus*: pimps (French); *literati*: writers and intellectuals.

with dubious means of subsistence and of dubious origin, alongside ruined and adventurous offshoots of the bourgeoisie, were vagabonds, discharged soldiers, discharged jailbirds, escaped galley slaves, swindlers, mountebanks, *lazzaroni*, pickpockets, tricksters, gamblers, *maquereaus*, brothel keepers, porters, *literati*, organ-grinders, ragpickers, knife grinders, tinkers, beggars—in short, the whole indefinite, disintegrated mass, thrown hither and thither, which the French term *la bohème*; from this kindred element Bona-parte formed the core of the Society of December 10. A "benevolent society"—in so far as, like Bonaparte, all its members felt the need of benefiting themselves at the expense of the labouring nation. This Bonaparte, who constitutes himself *chief of the lumpenproletariat*, who here alone rediscovers in mass form the interests which he per-sonally pursues, who recognizes in this scum, offal, refuse of all classes the only class upon which he can base himself uncondition-ally, is the real Bonaparte, the Bonaparte *sans phrase.** An old crafty *roué*, he conceives the historical life of the nations and their per-formances of state as comedy in the most vulgar sense, as a mas-querade where the grand costumes, words and postures merely serve to mask the pettiest knavery. Thus on his expedition to Strasbourg, where a trained Swiss vulture had played the part of the Napoleonic eagle. For his irruption into Boulogne he puts some London lackeys into French uniforms. They represent the army. In his Society of De-cember 10, he assembles ten thousand rascally fellows, who are to play the part of the people, as Nick Bottom† that of the lion. At a mo-ment when the bourgeoisie itself played the most complete comedy, but in the most serious manner in the world, without infringing any of the pedantic conditions of French dramatic etiquette, and was it-self half deceived, half convinced of the solemnity of its own perfor-mance of state, the adventurer, who took the comedy as plain comedy, was bound to win. Only when he has eliminated his solemn opponent, when he himself now takes his imperial role seriously and under the Napoleonic mask imagines he is the real Napoleon, does he become the victim of his own conception of the world, the seri-ous buffoon who no longer takes world history for a comedy but his

---

*Without embellishment (French).
†Character in Shakespeare's *A Midsummer Night's Dream*.

comedy for world history. What the national *ateliers** were for the socialist workers, what the *Gardes mobiles* were for the bourgeois republicans, the Society of December 10 was for Bonaparte, the party fighting force peculiar to him. On his journeys the detachments of this society packing the railways had to improvise a public for him, stage public enthusiasm, roar *vive l'Empereur*,† insult and thrash republicans, of course, under the protection of the police. On his return journeys to Paris they had to form the advance guard, forestall counter-demonstrations or disperse them. The Society of December 10 belonged to him, it was *his* work, his very own idea. Whatever else he appropriates is put into his hands by the force of circumstances; whatever else he does, the circumstances do for him or he is content to copy from the deeds of others. But Bonaparte with official phrases about order, religion, family and property in public, before the citizens, and with the secret society of the Schufterles and Spiegelbergs,‡ the society of disorder, prostitution and theft, behind him—that is Bonaparte himself as original author, and the history of the Society of December 10 is his own history.

Now it had happened by way of exception that people's representatives belonging to the party of Order came under the cudgels of the Decembrists. Still more. Yon, the Police Commissioner assigned to the National Assembly and charged with watching over its safety, acting on the deposition of a certain Alais, advised the Permanent Commission that a section of the Decembrists had decided to assassinate General Changarnier and Dupin, the President of the National Assembly, and had already designated the individuals who were to perpetrate the deed. One comprehends the terror of M. Dupin. A parliamentary enquiry into the Society of December 10, that is, the profanation of the Bonapartist secret world, seemed inevitable. Just before the meeting of the National Assembly Bonaparte providently disbanded his society, naturally only on paper, for in a detailed memoir at the end of 1851 Police Prefect Carlier still sought in vain to move him to really break up the Decembrists.

---

*Ateliers: workshops (French); *Gardes mobiles:* mobile guards (French).
†Long live the emperor (French).
‡Immoral characters in the drama *Die Räuber*, by German writer Friedrich von Schiller (1759–1805). Marx thus alludes to dishonest elements within the party.

The Society of December 10 was to remain the private army of Bonaparte until he succeeded in transforming the public army into a Society of December 10. Bonaparte made the first attempt at this shortly after the adjournment of the National Assembly, and precisely with the money just wrested from it. As a fatalist, he lives in the conviction that there are certain higher powers which man, and the soldier in particular, cannot withstand. Among these powers he counts, first and foremost, cigars and champagne, cold poultry and garlic sausage. Accordingly, to begin with, he treats officers and non-commissioned officers in his Elysée apartments to cigars and champagne, to cold poultry and garlic sausage. On October 3 he repeats this manoeuvre with the mass of the troops at the St. Maur review, and on October 10 the same manoeuvre on a still larger scale at the Satory army parade. The Uncle remembered the campaigns of Alexander in Asia, the Nephew the triumphal marches of Bacchus in the same land. Alexander was a demigod, to be sure, but Bacchus was a god and moreover the tutelary deity of the Society of December 10.

After the review of October 3, the Permanent Commission summoned War Minister d'Hautpoul. He promised that these breaches of discipline should not recur. We know how on October 10 Bonaparte kept d'Hautpoul's word. As Commander-in-Chief of the Paris army, Changarnier had commanded at both reviews. He, at once a member of the Permanent Commission, chief of the National Guard, the "saviour" of January 29 and June 13, the "bulwark of society," the candidate of the party of Order for presidential honours, the suspected Monk of two monarchies, had hitherto never acknowledged himself as the subordinate of the War Minister, had always openly derided the republican Constitution and had pursued Bonaparte with an ambiguous lordly protection. Now he was consumed with zeal for discipline against the War Minister and for the Constitution against Bonaparte. While on October 10 a section of the cavalry raised the shout: "*Vive Napoléon! Vivent les saucissons!*"* Changarnier arranged that at least the infantry marching past under the command of his friend Neumayer should preserve an icy silence. As a punishment, the War Minister relieved General Neumayer of his post in Paris at Bonaparte's instigation, on the pretext of ap-

---

*Hurrah for Napoleon! Hurrah for the sausages! (French).

pointing him commanding general of the fourteenth and fifteenth military divisions. Neumayer refused this exchange of posts and so had to resign. Changarnier, for his part, published an order of the day on November 2, in which he forbade the troops to indulge in political outcries or demonstrations of any kind while under arms. The Elysée newspapers* attacked Changarnier; the papers of the party of Order attacked Bonaparte; the Permanent Commission held repeated secret sessions in which it was repeatedly proposed to declare the country in danger; the army seemed divided into two hostile camps, with two hostile general staffs, one in the Elysée, where Bonaparte resided, the other in the Tuileries, the quarters of Changarnier. It seemed that only the meeting of the National Assembly was needed to give the signal for battle. The French public judged this friction between Bonaparte and Changarnier like that English journalist who characterized it in the following words:

> "The political housemaids of France are sweeping away the glowing lava of the revolution with old brooms and wrangle with one another while they do their work."

Meanwhile, Bonaparte hastened to remove the War Minister, d'Hautpoul, to pack him off in all haste to Algiers and to appoint General Schramm War Minister in his place. On November 12, he sent to the National Assembly a message of American prolixity, overloaded with detail, redolent of order, desirous of reconciliation, constitutionally acquiescent, treating of all and sundry, but not of the *questions brûlantes*† of the moment. As if in passing, he made the remark that according to the express provisions of the Constitution the President alone could dispose of the army. The message closed with the following words of great solemnity:

> "*Above all things, France demands tranquillity. . . . But bound by an oath, I shall keep within the narrow limits that it has set for me. . . .* As far as I am concerned, elected by the people and owing my power to

---

*Newspapers aligned with Bonaparte.
†Burning questions (French).

it alone, I shall always bow to its lawfully expressed will. Should you resolve at this session on a revision of the Constitution, a Constituent Assembly will regulate the position of the executive power. If not, then the people will solemnly pronounce its decision in 1852. But whatever the solutions of the future may be, let us come to an understanding, so that passion, surprise or violence may never decide the destiny of a great nation. . . . What occupies my attention, above all, is not who will rule France in 1852, but how to employ the time which remains at my disposal so that the intervening period may pass by without agitation or disturbance. I have opened my heart to you with sincerity; you will answer my frankness with your trust, my good endeavours with your cooperation, and God will do the rest."

The respectable, hypocritically moderate, virtuously commonplace language of the bourgeoisie reveals its deepest meaning in the mouth of the autocrat of the Society of December 10 and the picnic hero of St. Maur and Satory.

The burgraves of the party of Order did not delude themselves for a moment concerning the trust that this opening of the heart deserved. About oaths they had long been *blasé*; they numbered in their midst veterans and virtuosos of political perjury. Nor had they failed to hear the passage about the army. They observed with annoyance that in its discursive enumeration of lately enacted laws the message passed over the most important law, the electoral law, in studied silence, and, moreover, in the event of there being no revision of the Constitution, left the election of the President in 1852 to the people. The electoral law was the leaden ball chained to the feet of the party of Order, which prevented it from walking and so much the more from storming forward! Moreover, by the official disbandment of the Society of December 10 and the dismissal of the War Minister d'Hautpoul, Bonaparte had with his own hand sacrificed the scapegoats on the altar of the country. He had blunted the edge of the expected collision. Finally, the party of Order itself anxiously sought to avoid, to mitigate, to gloss over any decisive conflict with the executive power. For fear of losing their conquests over the revolution, they allowed their rival to carry off the fruits thereof. "Above all things, France demands tranquillity." This was what the party of Order had cried to the revolution since February, this was what

Bonaparte's message cried to the party of Order. "Above all things, France demands tranquillity." Bonaparte committed acts that aimed at usurpation, but the party of Order committed "unrest" if it raised a row about these acts and construed them hypochondriacally. The sausages of Satory were quiet as mice when no one spoke of them. "Above all things, France demands tranquillity." Bonaparte demanded, therefore, that he be left in peace to do as he liked and the parliamentary party was paralyzed by a double fear, by the fear of again evoking revolutionary unrest and by the fear of itself appearing as the instigator of unrest in the eyes of its own class, in the eyes of the bourgeoisie. Consequently, since France demanded tranquillity above all things, the party of Order dared not answer "war" after Bonaparte had talked "peace" in his message. The public, which had anticipated scenes of great scandal at the opening of the National Assembly, was cheated of its expectations. The opposition deputies, who demanded the submission of the Permanent Commission's minutes on the October events, were outvoted by the majority. On principle, all debates that might cause excitement were eschewed. The proceedings of the National Assembly during November and December 1850 were without interest.

At last, towards the end of December, guerilla warfare began over a number of prerogatives of parliament. The movement got bogged in petty squabbles regarding the prerogatives of the two powers, since the bourgeoisie had done away with the class struggle for the moment by abolishing universal suffrage.

A judgment for debt had been obtained from the court against Mauguin, one of the People's Representatives. In answer to the enquiry of the President of the Court, the Minister of Justice, Rouher, declared that a *capias** should be issued against the debtor without further ado. Mauguin was thus thrown into the debtors' jail. The National Assembly flared up when it learned of the assault. Not only did it order his immediate release, but it even had him fetched forcibly from Clichy the same evening, by its *greffier.*† In order, however, to confirm its faith in the sanctity of private property and with the idea at the back of its mind of opening, in case of need, an asylum for

---

*Arrest warrant (Latin).
†Clerk (French).

Montagnards who had become troublesome, it declared imprisonment of People's Representatives for debt permissible after previously
obtaining its consent. It forgot to decree that the President might also
be locked up for debt. It destroyed the last semblance of the immunity that enveloped the members of its own body.

It will be remembered that, acting on the information given by a
certain Alais, Police Commissioner Yon had denounced a section of
the Decembrists for planning the murder of Dupin and Changarnier. In reference to this, at the very first sitting the quaestors made
the proposal that parliament should form a police force of its own,
paid out of the private budget of the National Assembly and absolutely independent of the police prefect. The Minister of the Interior, Baroche, protested against this invasion of his domain. A
miserable compromise on this matter was concluded, according to
which, true, the police commissioner of the Assembly was to be paid
out of its private budget and to be appointed and dismissed by its
quaestors, but only after previous agreement with the Minister of
the Interior. Meanwhile criminal proceedings had been taken by the
government against Alais, and here it was easy to represent his information as a hoax and through the mouth of the public prosecutor to cast ridicule upon Dupin, Changarnier, Yon and the whole
National Assembly. Thereupon, on December 29, Minister Baroche
writes a letter to Dupin in which he demands Yon's dismissal. The
Bureau of the National Assembly decides to retain Yon in his position, but the National Assembly, alarmed by its violence in the Mauguin affair and accustomed when it has ventured a blow at the
executive power to receive two blows from it in return, does not
sanction this decision. It dismisses Yon as a reward for his official
zeal and robs itself of a parliamentary prerogative indispensable
against a man who does not decide by night in order to execute by
day, but who decides by day and executes by night.

We have seen how on great and striking occasions during the
months of November and December the National Assembly avoided
or quashed the struggle with the executive power. Now we see it
compelled to take it up on the pettiest occasions. In the Mauguin affair it confirms the principle of imprisoning People's Representatives
for debt, but reserves the right to have it applied only to representatives obnoxious to itself and wrangles over this infamous privilege

with the Minister of Justice. Instead of availing itself of the alleged murder plot to decree an enquiry into the Society of December 10 and irredeemably unmasking Bonaparte before France and Europe in his true character of chief of the Paris *lumpenproletariat,* it lets the conflict be degraded to a point where the only issue between it and the Minister of the Interior is which of them has the authority to appoint and dismiss a police commissioner. Thus, during the whole of this period, we see the party of Order compelled by its equivocal position to dissipate and disintegrate its struggle with the executive power in petty jurisdictional squabbles, petty-foggery, legalistic hairsplitting, and delimitational disputes, and to make the most ridiculous matters of form the substance of its activity. It does not dare to take up the conflict at the moment when this has significance from the standpoint of principle, when the executive power has really exposed itself and the cause of the National Assembly would be the cause of the nation. By so doing it would give the nation its marching orders, and it fears nothing more than that the nation should move. On such occasions it accordingly rejects the motions of the *Montagne* and proceeds to the order of the day. The question at issue in its larger aspects having thus been dropped, the executive power calmly bides the time when it can again take up the same question on petty and insignificant occasions, when this is, so to speak, of only local parliamentary interest. Then the repressed rage of the party of Order breaks out, then it tears away the curtain from the coulisses, then it denounces the President, then it declares the republic in danger, but then, also, its fervour appears absurd and the occasion for the struggle seems a hypocritical pretext or altogether not worth fighting about. The parliamentary storm becomes a storm in a teacup, the fight becomes an intrigue, the conflict a scandal. While the revolutionary classes gloat with malicious joy over the humiliation of the National Assembly, for they are just as enthusiastic about the parliamentary prerogatives of this Assembly as the latter is about the public liberties, the bourgeoisie outside parliament does not understand how the bourgeoisie inside parliament can waste time over such petty squabbles and imperil tranquillity by such pitiful rivalries with the President. It becomes confused by a strategy that makes peace at the moment when all the world is expecting battles, and attacks at the moment when all the world believes peace has been made.

On December 20, Pascal Duprat interpellated the Minister of the Interior concerning the Gold Bars Lottery. This lottery was a "daughter of Elysium."* Bonaparte with his faithful followers had brought her into the world and Police Prefect Carlier had placed her under his official protection, although French law forbids all lotteries with the exception of raffles for charitable purposes. Seven million lottery tickets at a franc apiece, the profits ostensibly to be devoted to shipping Parisian vagabonds to California. On the one hand, golden dreams were to supplant the socialist dreams of the Paris proletariat; the seductive prospect of the first prize, the doctrinaire right to work. Naturally, the Paris workers did not recognize in the glitter of the California gold bars the inconspicuous francs that were enticed out of their pockets. In the main, however, the matter was nothing short of a downright swindle. The vagabonds who wanted to open California gold mines without troubling to leave Paris were Bonaparte himself and his debt-ridden Round Table. The three millions voted by the National Assembly had been squandered in riotous living; in one way or another the coffers had to be replenished. In vain had Bonaparte opened a national subscription for the building of so-called *cités ouvrières*,† and figured at the head of the list himself with a considerable sum. The hardhearted bourgeois waited mistrustfully for him to pay up his share and since this, naturally, did not ensue, the speculation in socialist castles in the air fell straightway to the ground. The gold bars proved a better draw. Bonaparte & Co. were not content to pocket part of the excess of the seven millions over the bars to be allotted in prizes; they manufactured false lottery tickets; they issued ten, fifteen and even twenty tickets with the same number—a financial operation in the spirit of the Society of December 10! Here the National Assembly was confronted not with the fictitious President of the republic, but with Bonaparte in the flesh. Here it could catch him in the act, in conflict not with the Constitution but with the *Code*

---

*Marx puns on the name of the Champs Elysée (Elysian Fields), a major avenue in Paris, and the Palais Elysée, Louis Bonaparte's residence.
†Settlements for workers (French).

*pénal.** If on Duprat's interpellation it proceeded to the order of the day, this did not happen merely because Girardin's motion that it should declare itself "*satisfait*"† reminded the party of Order of its own systematic corruption. The bourgeois and, above all, the bourgeois inflated into a statesman, supplements his practical meanness by theoretical extravagance. As a statesman he becomes, like the state power that confronts him, a higher being that can only be fought in a higher, consecrated fashion.

Bonaparte, who precisely because he was a Bohemian, a princely *lumpenproletarian*, had the advantage over a rascally bourgeois in that he could conduct the struggle meanly, now saw, after the Assembly had itself guided him with its own hand across the slippery ground of the military banquets, the reviews, the Society of December 10, and, finally, the *Code pénal*, that the moment had come when he could pass from an apparent defensive to the offensive. The minor defeats meanwhile sustained by the Minister of Justice, the Minister of War, the Minister of the Navy and the Minister of Finance, through which the National Assembly signified its snarling displeasure, troubled him little. He not only prevented the ministers from resigning and thus recognizing the sovereignty of parliament over the executive power, but could now consummate what he had begun during the recess of the National Assembly: the severance of the military power from parliament, the *removal of Changarnier*.

An Elysée paper published an order of the day alleged to have been addressed during the month of May to the First Military Division, and therefore proceeding from Changarnier, in which the officers were recommended, in the event of an insurrection, to give no quarter to the traitors in their own ranks, but to shoot them immediately and refuse the National Assembly the troops, should it requisition them. On January 3, 1851, the Cabinet was interpellated concerning this order of the day. For the investigation of this matter it requests a breathing space, first of three months, then of a week, finally of only twenty-four hours. The Assembly insists on an immediate explanation. Changarnier rises and declares that there never was such an order of the day. He adds that he will always hasten to comply with

---

*Penal code (French).
†Satisfied (French).

the demands of the National Assembly and that in ease of a clash it can count on him. It receives his declaration with indescribable applause and passes a vote of confidence in him. It abdicates, it decrees its own impotence and the omnipotence of the army by placing itself under the private protection of a general; but the general deceives himself when he puts at its command against Bonaparte a power that he only holds as a fief from the same Bonaparte and when, in his turn, he expects to be protected by this parliament, by his own protégé in need of protection. Changarnier, however, believes in the mysterious power with which the bourgeoisie has endowed him since January 29, 1849. He considers himself the third power, existing side by side with both the other state powers. He shares the fate of the rest of this epoch's heroes, or rather saints, whose greatness consists precisely in the biassed great opinion of them that their party creates in its own interests and who shrink to everyday figures as soon as circumstances call on them to perform miracles. Unbelief is, in general, the mortal enemy of these reputed heroes and real saints. Hence their majestically moral indignation at the dearth of enthusiasm displayed by wits and scoffers.

The same evening, the ministers were summoned to the Elysée; Bonaparte insists on the dismissal of Changarnier; five ministers refuse to sign it; the *Moniteur* announces a ministerial crisis, and the press of the party of Order threatens to form a parliamentary army under Changarnier's command. The party of Order had constitutional authority to take this step. It merely had to appoint Changarnier President of the National Assembly and requisition any number of troops it pleased for its protection. It could do so all the more safely as Changarnier still actually stood at the head of the army and the Paris National Guard and was only waiting to be requisitioned together with the army. The Bonapartist press did not as yet even dare to question the right of the National Assembly directly to requisition troops, a legal scruple that in the given circumstances did not promise any success. That the army would have obeyed the orders of the National Assembly is probable when one bears in mind that Bonaparte had to search all Paris for eight days in order, finally, to find two generals—Baraguay d'Hilliers and Saint-Jean d'Angely—who declared themselves ready to countersign Changarnier's dismissal. That the party of Order, however, would have found in its own ranks and in parliament the necessary number of votes for such a resolution is more than doubtful, when one considers that eight days later two hundred and eighty-six votes detached themselves from the party and that in December 1851, at the last hour for decision, the *Montagne* still rejected a similar proposal. Nevertheless, the burgraves might, perhaps, still have succeeded in spurring the mass of their party to a heroism that consisted in feeling themselves secure behind a forest of bayonets and accepting the services of an army that had deserted to their camp. Instead of this, on the evening of January 6, Messrs. the Burgraves betook themselves to the Elysée in order to make Bonaparte desist from dismissing Changarnier by using statesmanlike phrases and urging considerations of state. Whomever one seeks to persuade, one acknowledges as master of the situation. On January 12, Bonaparte, assured by this step, appoints a new ministry in which the leaders of the old ministry, Fould and Baroche, remain. Saint-Jean d'Angely becomes War Minister, the *Moniteur* publishes the decree dismissing Changarnier, and his command is divided between Baraguay d'Hilliers, who receives the First Army Division, and Perrot, who receives the National Guard. The bulwark of society has been discharged, and while this does not cause any tiles to fall from the roofs, quotations on the *bourse* are, on the other hand, going up.

By repulsing the army, which places itself in the person of Changarnier at its disposal, and so surrendering the army irrevocably to the President, the party of Order declares that the bourgeoisie has forfeited its vocation to rule. A parliamentary ministry no longer existed. Having now indeed lost its grip on the army and National Guard, what forcible means remained to it with which simultaneously to maintain the usurped authority of parliament over the people and its constitutional authority against the President? None. Only the appeal to forceless principles remained to it now, to principles that it had itself always interpreted merely as general rules, which one prescribes for others in order to be able to move all the more freely oneself. The dismissal of Changarnier and the falling of the military power into Bonaparte's hands closes the first part of the period we are considering, the period of struggle between the party of Order and the executive power. War between the two powers has now been openly declared, is openly waged, but only after the party of Order has lost both arms and soldiers. Without the ministry, without the army, without the people, without public opinion, after its Electoral Law of May 31 no longer the representative of the sovereign nation, *sans* eyes, *sans* ears, *sans* teeth, *sans* everything, the National Assembly had undergone a gradual transformation into an *ancient French Parliament** that has to leave action to the government and content itself with growling remonstrances *post festum.*†

The party of Order receives the new ministry with a storm of indignation. General Bedeau recalls to mind the mildness of the Permanent Commission during the recess, and the excessive consideration it had shown by waiving the publication of its minutes. The Minister of the Interior now himself insists on the publication of these minutes, which by this time have naturally become as dull as ditch-water, disclose no fresh facts and have not the slightest effect on the *blasé* public. Upon Rémusat's proposal the National Assembly retires into its bureaux and appoints a "Committee for Extraordinary Measures." Paris departs the less from the rut of its everyday routine, since at this moment trade is prosperous, manufactories are busy, corn prices low, foodstuffs overflowing and the savings banks receive fresh deposits daily. The "extraordinary measures" that parliament has announced with so much noise fizzle out on January 18 in a no-confidence vote against the ministry without General Changarnier even being mentioned. The party of Order had been forced to frame its motion in this way in order to secure the votes of the republicans, as, of all the measures of the ministry, Changarnier's dismissal is precisely the only one which the republicans approve of, while the party of Order is in fact not in a position to censure the other ministerial acts, which it had itself dictated.

The no-confidence vote of January 18 was passed by four hundred and fifteen votes to two hundred and eighty-six. Thus, it was carried only by a *coalition* of the extreme Legitimists and Orleanists with the pure republicans and the *Montagne.* Thus it proved that the party of Order had lost in conflicts with Bonaparte not only the ministry, not only the army, but also its independent parliamentary majority, that a squad of representatives had deserted from its

---

*Older, weak form of parliament predating the French Revolution of 1789.
†Literally, after the feast (Latin); too late.

camp, out of fanaticism for conciliation, out of fear of the struggle, out of lassitude, out of family regard for the state salaries so near and dear to them, out of speculation on ministerial posts becoming vacant (Odilon Barrot), out of sheer egoism, which makes the ordinary bourgeois always inclined to sacrifice the general interest of his class for this or that private motive. From the first, the Bonapartist representatives adhered to the party of Order only in the struggle against revolution. The leader of the Catholic party, Montalembert, had already at that time thrown his influence into the Bonapartist scale, since he despaired of the parliamentary party's prospects of life. Lastly, the leaders of this party, Thiers and Berryer, the Orleanist and the Legitimist, were compelled openly to proclaim themselves republicans, to confess that their hearts were royalist but their heads republican, that the parliamentary republic was the sole possible form for the rule of the bourgeoisie as a whole. Thus they were compelled, before the eyes of the bourgeois class itself, to stigmatize the Restoration plans, which they continued indefatigably to pursue behind parliament's back as an intrigue as dangerous as it was brainless.

The no-confidence vote of January 18 hit the ministers and not the President. But it was not the ministry, it was the President who had dismissed Changarnier. Should the party of Order impeach Bonaparte himself? On account of his restoration desires? The latter merely supplemented their own. On account of his conspiracy in connection with the military reviews and the Society of December 10? They had buried these themes long since under simple orders of the day. On account of the dismissal of the hero of January 29 and June 13, the man who in May 1850 threatened to set fire to all four corners of Paris in the event of a rising? Their allies of the *Montagne* and Cavaignac did not even allow them to raise the fallen bulwark of society by means of an official attestation of sympathy. They themselves could not deny the President the constitutional authority to dismiss a general. They only raged because he made an unparliamentary use of his constitutional right. Had they not continually made an unconstitutional use of their parliamentary prerogative, particularly in regard to the abolition of universal suffrage? They were therefore reduced to moving within strictly parliamentary limits. And it took that peculiar malady which since 1848 has raged all over the Continent, *parliamentary cretinism*, which holds those infected by it fast in an imaginary world and robs them of all sense, all memory, all understanding of the rude external world—it took this parliamentary cretinism for those who had destroyed all the conditions of parliamentary power with their own hands, and were bound to destroy them in their struggle with the other classes, still to regard their parliamentary victories as victories and to believe they hit the President by striking at his ministers. They merely gave him the opportunity to humiliate the National Assembly afresh in the eyes of the nation. On January 20 the *Moniteur* announced that the resignation of the entire ministry had been accepted. On the pretext that no parliamentary party any longer had a majority, as the vote of January 18, this fruit of the coalition between *Montagne* and royalists, proved, and pending the formation of a new majority, Bonaparte appointed a so-called transition ministry, not one member of which was a member of parliament, all being absolutely unknown and insignificant individuals, a ministry of mere clerks and copyists. The party of Order could now work to exhaustion playing with these marionettes; the executive power no longer thought it worth while to be seriously represented in the National Assembly. The more his ministers were pure dummies, the more manifestly Bonaparte concentrated the whole executive power in his own person and the more scope he had to exploit it for his own ends.

In coalition with the *Montagne*, the party of Order revenged itself by rejecting the grant to the President of one million eight hundred thousand francs, which the chief of the Society of December 10 had compelled his ministerial clerks to propose. This time a majority of only a hundred and two votes decided the matter; thus twenty-seven fresh votes had fallen away since January 18; the dissolution of the party of Order was making progress. At the same time, in order that there might not for a moment be any mistake about the meaning of its coalition with the *Montagne*, it scorned even to consider a proposal signed by a hundred and eighty-nine members of the *Montagne* calling for a general amnesty of political offenders. It sufficed for the Minister of the Interior, a certain Vaïsse, to declare that the tranquillity was only apparent, that in secret great agitation prevailed, that in secret ubiquitous societies were being organized, the democratic papers were preparing to come out again, the reports from the Departments were unfavourable, the Geneva refugees were directing a conspiracy spreading by way of Lyons over all the south of France, France was on the verge of an industrial and commercial crisis, the manufacturers of Roubaix had reduced working hours, that the prisoners of Belle Isle* were in revolt—it sufficed for even a mere Vaïsse to conjure up the red spectre and the party of Order rejected without discussion a motion that would certainly have won the National Assembly immense popularity and thrown Bonaparte back into its arms. Instead of letting itself be intimidated by the executive power with the prospect of fresh disturbances, it ought rather to have allowed the class struggle a little elbowroom, so as to keep the executive power dependent on itself. But it did not feel equal to the task of playing with fire.

Meanwhile, the so-called transition ministry continued to vegetate until the middle of April. Bonaparte wearied and befooled the National Assembly with continual new ministerial combinations. Now he seemed to want to form a republican ministry with Lamartine and Billault, now a parliamentary one with the inevitable Odilon Barrot, whose name may never be missing when a dupe is necessary, then a Legitimist ministry with Vatimesnil and Benoit d'Azy, and then again an Orleanist one with Maleville. While he thus kept the different factions of the party of Order in tension against one another and alarmed them as a whole by the prospect of a republican ministry and the consequent inevitable restoration of universal suffrage, he at the same time engendered in the bourgeoisie the conviction that his honest efforts to form a parliamentary ministry were being frustrated by the irreconcilability of the royalist factions. The bourgeoisie, however, cried out all the louder for a "strong government"; it found it all the more unpardonable to leave France "without administration," the more a general commercial crisis seemed now to be approaching and won recruits for Socialism in the towns just as the ruinously low price of corn did in the countryside. Trade became daily slacker, the unemployed hands increased perceptibly, ten thousand workers, at least, were breadless in Paris, innumerable factories stood idle in Rouen, Mulhouse, Lyons, Roubaix, Tourcoing, St. Etienne, Elbeuf, etc. Under these circumstances Bona-

---

*Detention center for political prisoners, located on the west coast of France.

parte could venture, on April 11, to restore the ministry of January 18: Messers. Rouher, Fould, Baroche, etc., reinforced by M. Léon Faucher, whom the Constituent Assembly during its last days had, with the exception of five votes cast by ministers, unanimously stigmatized by a vote of no-confidence for sending out false telegrams. The National Assembly had therefore gained a victory over the ministry on January 18, had struggled with Bonaparte for three months, only to have Fould and Baroche on April 11 admit the puritan Faucher as a third party into their ministerial alliance.

In November 1849, Bonaparte had contented himself with an *unparliamentary* ministry, in January 1851 with an *extra-parliamentary* one, and on April 11 he felt strong enough to form an *anti-parliamentary* ministry, which harmoniously combined in itself the no-confidence votes of both Assemblies, the Constituent and the Legislative, the republican and the royalist. This gradation of ministries was the thermometer with which parliament could measure the decrease of its own vital heat. By the end of April the latter had fallen so low that Persigny, in a personal interview, could urge Changarnier to go over to the camp of the President. Bonaparte, he assured him, regarded the influence of the National Assembly as completely destroyed, and the proclamation was already prepared that was to be published after the *coup d'état*, which was kept steadily in view but was by chance again postponed. Changarnier informed the leaders of the party of Order of the obituary notice, but who believes that bedbug bites are fatal? And parliament, stricken, disintegrated and death-tainted as it was, could not prevail upon itself to see in its duel with the grotesque chief of the Society of December 10 anything but a duel with a bedbug. But Bonaparte answered the party of Order as Agesilaus did King Agis:

"*I seem to thee an ant, but one day I shall be a lion.*"*

---

*Marx alludes to the Spartan king Agesilaus, who was of small stature, as recounted by the Greek writer Athenaeus in his *Deipnosophistae*.

VI

THE COALITION WITH THE *Montagne* and the pure republicans, to which the party of Order saw itself condemned in its unavailing efforts to maintain possession of the military power and to reconquer supreme control of the executive power, proved incontrovertibly that it had forfeited its independent *parliamentary majority*. On May 28, the mere power of the calendar, of the hour hand of the clock, gave the signal for its complete disintegration. With May 28, the last year of the life of the National Assembly began. It had now to decide for continuing the Constitution unaltered or for revising it. But revision of the Constitution, that implied not only rule of the bourgeoisie or of the petty-bourgeois democracy, democracy or proletarian anarchy, parliamentary republic or Bonaparte, it implied at the same time Orleans or Bourbon! Thus fell in the midst of parliament the apple of discord that was bound to inflame openly the conflict of interests which split the party of Order into hostile factions. The party of Order was a combination of heterogeneous social substances. The question of revision generated a political temperature at which the product again decomposed into its original constituents.

The interest of the Bonapartists in a revision was simple. For them it was above all a question of abolishing Article 45, which forbade Bonaparte's re-election and the prolongation of his authority. No less simple appeared the position of the republicans. They unconditionally rejected any revision; they saw in it a universal conspiracy against the republic. Since they commanded *more than a quarter of the votes* in the National Assembly and, according to the Constitution, three-quarters of the votes were required for a resolution for revision to be legally valid and for the convocation of a revising Assembly, they only needed to count their votes to be sure of victory. And they were sure of victory.

As against these clear positions, the party of Order found itself caught in inextricable contradictions. If it should reject revision, it would imperil the *status quo*, since it would leave Bonaparte only one way out, that of force, and since on the second Sunday in May

1852, at the decisive moment, it would be surrendering France to revolutionary anarchy, with a President who had lost his authority, with a parliament which for a long time had not possessed it and with a people that meant to reconquer it. If it voted for constitutional revision, it knew that it voted in vain and would be bound to fail constitutionally because of the veto of the republicans. If it unconstitutionally declared a simple majority vote to be binding, then it could hope to dominate the revolution only if it subordinated itself unconditionally to the sovereignty of the executive power, then it would make Bonaparte master of the Constitution, of its revision and of itself. Only a partial revision which would prolong the authority of the President would pave the way for imperial usurpation. A general revision which would shorten the existence of the republic would bring the dynastic claims into unavoidable conflict, for the conditions of a Bourbon and the conditions of an Orleanist Restoration were not only different, they were mutually exclusive.

The parliamentary republic was more than the neutral territory on which the two factions of the French bourgeoisie, Legitimists and Orleanists, large landed property and industry, could dwell side by side with equality of rights. It was the unavoidable condition of their *common* rule, the sole form of state in which their general class interest subjected to itself at the same time both the claims of their particular factions and all the remaining classes of society. As royalists they fell back into their old antagonism, into the struggle for the supremacy of landed property or of money, and the highest expression of this antagonism, its personification, was their kings themselves, their dynasties. Hence the resistance of the party of Order to the *recall of the Bourbons*.

The Orleanist and people's representative Creton had in 1849, 1850 and 1851 periodically introduced a motion for the revocation of the decree exiling the royal families. Just as regularly parliament presented the spectacle of an Assembly of royalists that obdurately barred the gates through which their exiled kings might return home. Richard III had murdered Henry VI, remarking that he was too good for this world and belonged in heaven. They declared France too bad to possess her kings again. Constrained by force of circumstances, they had become republicans and repeatedly sanctioned the popular decision that banished their kings from France.

A revision of the Constitution—and circumstances compelled taking it into consideration—called in question, along with the republic, the common rule of the two bourgeois factions, and revived, with the possibility of a monarchy, the rivalry of the interests which it had predominantly represented by turns, the struggle for the supremacy of one faction over the other. The diplomats of the party of Order believed they could settle the struggle by an amalgamation of the two dynasties, by a so-called *fusion* of the royalist parties and their royal houses. The real fusion of the Restoration and the July Monarchy was the parliamentary republic, in which Orleanist and Legitimist colours were obliterated and the various species of bourgeois disappeared in the bourgeois as such, in the bourgeois genus. Now, however, Orleanist was to become Legitimist and Legitimist Orleanist. Royalty, in which their antagonism was personified, was to embody their unity; the expression of their exclusive factional interests was to become the expression of their common class interest; the monarchy was to do that which only the abolition of two monarchies, the republic, could do and had done. This was the philosopher's stone, to produce which the doctors of the party of Order racked their brains. As if the Legitimist monarchy could ever become the monarchy of the industrial bourgeois or the bourgeois monarchy ever become the monarchy of the hereditary landed aristocracy. As if landed property and industry could fraternize under *one* crown, when the crown could only descend to one head, the head of the elder brother or of the younger. As if industry could come to terms with landed property at all, so long as landed property does not decide itself to become industrial. If Henry V should die tomorrow, the Count of Paris would not on that account become the king of the Legitimists unless he ceased to be the king of the Orleanists. The philosophers of fusion, however, who became more vociferous in proportion as the question of revision came to the fore, who had provided themselves with an official daily organ in the *Assemblée Nationale* and who are again at work even at this very moment (February 1852), considered the whole difficulty to be due to the opposition and rivalry of the two dynasties. The attempts to reconcile the Orleans family with Henry V, begun since the death of Louis Philippe, but, like the dynastic intrigues generally, played at only while the National Assembly was in recess, during the

*entr'actes,** behind the scenes, sentimental coquetry with the old superstition rather than seriously-meant business, now became grand
performances of state, enacted by the party of Order on the public
stage, instead of in amateur theatricals, as hitherto. The couriers
sped from Paris to Venice,† from Venice to Claremont, from Claremont to Paris. The Count of Chambord issues a manifesto in which
"with the help of all the members of his family" he announces not
his, but the "national" Restoration. The Orleanist Salvandy throws
himself at the feet of Henry V. The Legitimist chiefs, Berryer, Benoit
d'Azy, Saint-Priest, travel to Claremont in order to persuade the Orleans set, but in vain. The fusionists perceive too late that the interests of the two bourgeois factions neither lose exclusiveness nor gain
pliancy when they become accentuated in the form of family interests, the interests of two royal houses. If Henry V were to recognize
the Count of Paris as his successor—the sole success that the fusion
could achieve at best—the House of Orleans would not win any
claim that the childlessness of Henry V had not already secured to it,
but it would lose all claims that it had gained through the July Revolution. It would waive its original claims, all the titles that it had
wrested from the older branch of the Bourbons in almost a hundred
years of struggle; it would barter away its historical prerogative, the
prerogative of the modern kingdom, for the prerogative of its ge-
nealogical tree. The fusion, therefore, would be nothing but a vol-
untary abdication of the House of Orleans, its resignation to
Legitimacy, repentant withdrawal from the Protestant state church
into the Catholic. A withdrawal, moreover, that would not even
bring it to the throne which it had lost, but to the throne's steps, on
which it had been born. The old Orleanist ministers, Guizot, Duchâ-
tel, etc., who likewise hastened to Claremont to advocate the fusion,
in fact represented merely the *Katzenjammer*‡ over the July Revolution, the despair felt in regard to the bourgeois kingdom and the
kingliness of the bourgeois, the superstitious belief in Legitimacy as
the last charm against anarchy. Imagining themselves mediators be-

---

*Interludes of dance or music performed during intermission (French).
†City where Henri-Dieudonné d'Artois, count de Chambord, the Legitimist pre-
tender to the French throne, lived (see footnote on p. 93).
‡Hangover (German).

tween Orleans and Bourbons, they were in reality merely Orleanist renegades, and the prince of Joinville received them as such. On the other hand, the viable, bellicose section of the Orleanists, Thiers, Baze, etc., convinced Louis Philippe's family all the more easily that if any directly monarchist restoration presupposed the fusion of the two dynasties and if any such fusion, however, presupposed abdication of the House of Orleans, it was, on the contrary, wholly in accord with the tradition of their forefathers to recognize the republic for the moment and wait until events permitted the conversion of the presidential chair into a throne. Rumours of Joinville's candidature were circulated, public curiosity was kept in suspense and, a few months later, in September, after the rejection of revision, his candidature was publicly proclaimed.

The attempt at a royalist fusion of Orleanists with Legitimists had thus not only failed; it had destroyed their *parliamentary fusion*, their common republican form, and had broken up the party of Order into its original component parts; but the more the estrangement between Claremont and Venice grew, the more their settlement broke down and the Joinville agitation gained ground, so much the more eager and earnest became the negotiations between Bonaparte's minister Faucher and the Legitimists.

The disintegration of the party of Order did not stop at its original elements. Each of the two great factions, in its turn, underwent decomposition anew. It was as if all the old nuances that had formerly fought and jostled one another within each of the two circles, whether Legitimist or Orleanist, had thawed out again like dry Infusoria on contact with water, as if they had acquired anew sufficient vital energy to form groups of their own and independent antagonisms. The Legitimists dreamed that they were back among the controversies between the Tuileries and the Pavillon Marsan, between Villèle and Polignac. The Orleanists relived the golden days of the tourneys between Guizot, Molé, Broglie, Thiers and Odilon Barrot.*

That part of the party of Order which was eager for revision, but was divided again on the limits to revision, a section composed of the Legitimists led by Berryer and Falloux, on the one hand, and by

---

*Marx refers to the conflicts between the Legitimists and the Orleanists during the Restoration in France, from 1814 to 1830.

La Rochejaquelein, on the other, and of the conflict-weary Orleanists led by Molé, Broglie, Montalembert and Odilon Barrot,
agreed with the Bonapartist representatives on the following indefinite and broadly framed motion:

> "With the object of restoring to the nation the full exercise of its sov-
> ereignty, the undersigned Representatives move that the Constitution
> be revised."

At the same time, however, they unanimously declared through
their reporter Tocqueville that the National Assembly had not the
right to move the *abolition of the republic,* that this right was vested
solely in the Revising Chamber. For the rest, the Constitution might
be revised only in a *"legal" manner,* hence only if the constitutionally prescribed three-quarters of the number of votes were cast in
favour of revision. On July 19, after six days of stormy debate, revision was rejected, as was to be anticipated. Four hundred and forty-
six votes were cast for it, but two hundred and seventy-eight against.
The extreme Orleanists, Thiers, Changarnier, etc., voted with the republicans and the *Montagne.*

Thus the majority of parliament declared against the Constitution, but this Constitution itself declared for the minority and that
its vote was binding. But had not the party of Order subordinated
the Constitution to the parliamentary majority on May 31, 1850,
and on June 13, 1849? Up to now, was not its whole policy based on
the subordination of the paragraphs of the Constitution to the decisions of the parliamentary majority? Had it not left to the democrats
the antediluvian superstitious belief in the letter of the law, and castigated the democrats for it? At the present moment, however, revision of the Constitution meant nothing but continuation of the
presidential authority, just as continuation of the Constitution
meant nothing but Bonaparte's deposition. Parliament had declared
for him, but the Constitution declared against parliament. He therefore acted in the sense of parliament when he tore up the Constitution and he acted in the sense of the Constitution when he dispersed
parliament.

Parliament had declared the Constitution and, with the latter, its
own rule to be "beyond the majority"; by its vote it had abolished the

Constitution and prolonged the term of presidential power, while declaring at the same time that neither can the one die nor the other live so long as it itself continues to exist. Those who were to bury it were standing at the door. While it debated on revision, Bonaparte removed General Baraguay d'Hilliers, who had proved irresolute, from the command of the First Army Division and appointed in his place General Magnan, the victor of Lyons, the hero of the December days, one of his creatures, who under Louis Philippe had already compromised himself more or less in Bonaparte's favour on the occasion of the Boulogne expedition.

The party of Order proved by its decision on revision that it knew neither how to rule nor how to serve; neither how to live nor how to die; neither how to suffer the republic nor how to overthrow it; neither how to uphold the Constitution nor how to throw it overboard; neither how to cooperate with the President nor how to break with him. To whom, then, did it look for the solution of all the contradictions? To the calendar, to the course of events. It ceased to presume to sway the events. It therefore challenged the events to assume sway over it, and thereby challenged the power to which in the struggle against the people it had surrendered one attribute after another until it itself stood impotent before this power. In order that the head of the executive power might be able the more undisturbedly to draw up his plan of campaign against it, strengthen his means of attack, select his tools and fortify his positions, it resolved precisely at this critical moment to retire from the stage and adjourn for three months, from August 10 to November 4.

The parliamentary party was not only dissolved into its two great factions, each of these factions was not only split up within itself, but the party of Order in parliament had fallen out with the party of Order *outside* parliament. The spokesmen and scribes of the bourgeoisie, its platform and its press, in short, the ideologists of the bourgeoisie and the bourgeoisie itself, the representatives and the represented, faced one another in estrangement and no longer understood one another.

The Legitimists in the provinces, with their limited horizon and their unlimited enthusiasm, accused their parliamentary leaders, Berryer and Falloux, of deserting to the Bonapartist camp and of defection from Henry V. Their *fleur-de-lis** minds believed in the fall of man, but not in diplomacy.

Far more fateful and decisive was the breach of the commercial bourgeoisie with its politicians. It reproached them, not as the Legitimists reproached theirs, with having abandoned their principles, but, on the contrary, with clinging to principles that had become useless.

I have already indicated above that since Fould's entry into the ministry the section of the commercial bourgeoisie which had held the lion's share of power under Louis Philippe, namely, the *aristocracy of finance*, had become Bonapartist. Fould represented not only Bonaparte's interests in the *bourse*, he represented at the same time the interests of the *bourse* before Bonaparte. The position of the aristocracy of finance is most strikingly depicted in a passage from its European organ, the London *Economist*. In its number of February 1, 1851, its Paris correspondent writes:

> "Now we have it stated from numerous quarters that above all things France demands tranquillity. The President declares it in his message to the Legislative Assembly; it is echoed from the tribune; it is asserted in the journals; it is announced from the pulpit; *it is demonstrated by the sensitiveness of the public funds at the least prospect of disturbance, and their firmness the instant it is made manifest that the executive is victorious.*"

In its issue of November 29, 1851, *The Economist* declares in its own name:

> "*The President is the guardian of order, and is now recognized as such on every Stock Exchange of Europe.*"

The aristocracy of finance, therefore, condemned the parliamentary struggle of the party of Order with the executive power as a *disturbance of order*, and celebrated every victory of the President over its ostensible representatives as a *victory of order*. By the aristocracy of finance must here be understood not merely the great loan promoters and speculators in public funds, in regard to whom it is im-

---

*Emblem of the Bourbon dynasty, which features a stylized lily.

mediately obvious that their interests coincide with the interests of the state power. All modern finance, the whole of the banking business, is interwoven in the closest fashion with public credit. A part of their business capital is necessarily invested and put out at interest in quickly convertible public funds. Their deposits, the capital placed at their disposal and distributed by them among merchants and industrialists, are partly derived from the dividends of holders of government securities. If in every epoch the stability of the state power signified Moses and the prophets to the entire money market and to the priests of this money market, why not all the more so today, when every deluge threatens to sweep away the old states, and the old state debts with them?

The *industrial bourgeoisie*, too, in its fanaticism for order, was angered by the squabbles of the parliamentary party of Order with the executive power. After their vote of January 18 on the occasion of Changarnier's dismissal, Thiers, Anglès, Sainte-Beuve, etc., received from their constituents, in precisely the industrial districts, public reproofs in which particularly their coalition with the *Montagne* was scourged as high treason to order. If, as we have seen, the boastful taunts, the petty intrigues which marked the struggle of the party of Order with the President merited no better reception, then, on the other hand, this bourgeois party, which required its representatives to allow the military power to pass from its own parliament to an adventurous pretender without offering resistance, was not even worth the intrigues that were squandered in its interests. It proved that the struggle to maintain its *public* interests, its own *class interests*, its *political power*, only troubled and upset it, as it was a disturbance of private business.

With barely an exception, the bourgeois dignitaries of the Departmental towns, the municipal authorities, the judges of the Commercial Courts, etc., everywhere received Bonaparte on his tours in the most servile manner, even when, as in Dijon, he made an unrestrained attack on the National Assembly, and especially on the party of Order.

When trade was good, as it still was at the beginning of 1851, the commercial bourgeoisie raged against any parliamentary struggle, lest trade be put out of humour. When trade was bad, as it continually was from the end of February 1851, the commercial bourgeoisie accused the parliamentary struggles of being the cause of stagnation and cried out for them to stop in order that trade might start again. The revision debates came on just in this bad period. Since the question here was whether the existing form of state was to be or not to be, the bourgeoisie felt itself all the more justified in demanding from its Representatives the ending of this torturous provisional arrangement and at the same time the maintenance of the *status quo*. There was no contradiction in this. By the end of the provisional arrangement it understood precisely its continuation, the postponement to a distant future of the moment when a decision had to be reached. The *status quo* could be maintained in only two ways: prolongation of Bonaparte's authority or his constitutional retirement and the election of Cavaignac. A section of the bourgeoisie desired the latter solution and knew no better advice to give its Representatives than to keep silent and leave the burning question untouched. They were of the opinion that if their Representatives did not speak, Bonaparte would not act. They wanted an ostrich parliament that would hide its head in order to remain unseen. Another section of the bourgeoisie desired, because Bonaparte was already in the presidential chair, to leave him sitting in it, so that everything might remain in the same old rut. They were indignant because their parliament did not openly infringe the Constitution and abdicate without ceremony.

The General Councils of the Departments, those provincial representative bodies of the big bourgeoisie, which met from August 25 on during the recess of the National Assembly, declared almost unanimously for revision, and thus against parliament and in favour of Bonaparte.

Still more unequivocally than in its falling out with its *parliamentary representatives* the bourgeoisie displayed its wrath against its literary representatives, its own press. The sentences to ruinous fines and shameless terms of imprisonment, on the verdicts of bourgeois juries, for every attack of bourgeois journalists on Bonaparte's usurpationist desires, for every attempt of the press to defend the political rights of the bourgeoisie against the executive power, astonished not merely France, but all Europe.

While the *parliamentary party of Order*, by its clamour for tranquillity, as I have shown, committed itself to quiescence, while it declared the political rule of the bourgeoisie to be incompatible with the safety and existence of the bourgeoisie, by destroying with its own hands in the struggle against the other classes of society all the conditions for its own regime, the parliamentary regime, the *extra-parliamentary mass of the bourgeoisie,* on the other hand, by its servility towards the President, by its vilification of parliament, by its brutal maltreatment of its own press, invited Bonaparte to suppress and annihilate its speaking and writing section, its politicians and its *literati*, its platform and its press, in order that it might then be able to pursue its private affairs with full confidence in the protection of a strong and unrestricted government. It declared unequivocally that it longed to get rid of its own political rule in order to get rid of the troubles and dangers of ruling.

And this extra-parliamentary bourgeoisie, which had already rebelled against the purely parliamentary and literary struggle for the rule of its own class and betrayed the leaders of this struggle, now dares after the event to indict the proletariat for not having risen in a bloody struggle, a life-and-death struggle on its behalf! This bourgeoisie, which every moment sacrificed its general class interests, that is, its political interests, to the narrowest and most sordid private interests, and demanded a similar sacrifice from its Representatives, now moans that the proletariat has sacrificed its [the bourgeoisie's] ideal political interests to its [the proletariat's] material interests. It poses as a lovely being that has been misunderstood and deserted in the decisive hour by the proletariat misled by Socialists. And it finds a general echo in the bourgeois world. Naturally, I do not speak here of German shyster politicians and riffraff of the same persuasion. I refer, for example, to the already quoted *Economist*, which as late as November 29, 1851, that is, four days prior to the *coup d'état*, had declared Bonaparte to be the "guardian of order," but the Thiers and Berryers to be "anarchists," and on December 27, 1851, after Bonaparte had quieted these anarchists, is already vociferous concerning the treason to "the skill, knowledge, discipline, mental influence, intellectual resources and moral weight of the middle and upper ranks" committed by the masses of "ignorant, untrained, and stupid *proletaires.*" The stupid, ignorant and vulgar mass was none other than the bourgeois mass itself.

In the year 1851, France, to be sure, had passed through a kind of minor trade crisis. The end of February showed a decline in exports compared with 1850; in March trade suffered and factories closed down; in April the position of the industrial Departments appeared as desperate as after the February days; in May business had still not revived; as late as June 28 the holdings of the Bank of France showed, by the enormous growth of deposits and the equally great decrease in advances on bills of exchange, that production was at a standstill, and it was not until the middle of October that a progressive improvement of business again set in. The French bourgeoisie attributed this trade stagnation to purely political causes, to the struggle between parliament and the executive power, to the precariousness of a merely provisional form of state, to the terrifying prospect of the second Sunday in May 1852. I will not deny that all these circumstances had a depressing effect on some branches of industry in Paris and the Departments. But in any case this influence of the political conditions was only local and inconsiderable. Does this require further proof than the fact that the improvement of trade set in towards the middle of October, at the very moment when the political situation grew worse, the political horizon darkened and a thunderbolt from Elysium was expected at any moment? For the rest, the French bourgeois, whose "skill, knowledge, spiritual insight and intellectual resources" reach no further than his nose, could throughout the period of the Industrial Exhibition in London have found the cause of his commercial misery right under his nose. While in France factories were closed down, in England commercial bankruptcies broke out. While in April and May the industrial panic reached a climax in France, in April and May the commercial panic reached a climax in England. Like the French woollen industry, so the English woollen industry suffered, and as French silk manufacture, so did English silk manufacture. True, the English cotton mills continued working, but no longer at the same profits as in 1849 and 1850. The only difference was that the crisis in France was industrial, in England commercial; that while in France the factories stood idle, in England they extended operations, but under less favourable conditions than in preceding years; that in France it was exports, in England imports which were hardest hit. The common cause, which is naturally not to be sought within the bounds of the French political horizon, was obvious. The years 1849 and 1850 were years of the greatest material prosperity and of an overproduction that appeared as such only in 1851. At the beginning of this year it was given a further special impetus by the prospect of the Industrial Exhibition. In addition there were the following special circumstances: first, the partial failure of the cotton crop in 1850 and 1851, then the certainty of a bigger cotton crop than had been expected; first the rise, then the sudden fall, in short, the fluctuations in the price of cotton. The crop of raw silk, in France at least, had turned out to be even below the average yield. Woollen manufacture, finally, had expanded so much since 1848 that the production of wool could not keep pace with it and the price of raw wool rose out of all proportion to the price of woollen manufactures. Here, then, in the raw material of three industries for the world market, we have already threefold material for a stagnation in trade. Apart from these special circumstances, the apparent crisis of 1851 was nothing else but the halt which over-production and over-speculation invariably make in describing the industrial cycle, before they summon all their strength in order to rush feverishly through the final phase of this cycle and arrive once more at their starting-point, the *general trade crisis.* During such intervals in the history of trade, commercial bankruptcies break out in England, while in France industry itself is reduced to idleness, being partly forced into retreat by the competition, just then becoming intolerable, of the English in all markets, and being partly singled out for attack as a luxury industry by every business stagnation. Thus, besides the general crisis, France goes through national trade crises of her own, which are nevertheless determined and conditioned far more by the general state of the world market than by French local influences. It will not be without interest to contrast the judgment of the English bourgeois with the prejudice of the French bourgeois. In its annual trade report for 1851, one of the largest Liverpool houses writes:

"Few years have more thoroughly belied the anticipations formed at their commencement than the one just closed; instead of the great prosperity which was almost unanimously looked for it has proved one of the most discouraging that has been seen for the last quarter of a century—this, of course, refers to the mercantile, not to the manufacturing classes. And yet there certainly were grounds for anticipating the reverse at the beginning of the year—stocks of produce were moderate, money was abundant, and food was cheap, a plentiful harvest well secured, unbroken peace on the Continent, and no political or fiscal disturbances at home; indeed, the wings of commerce were never more unfettered. . . . To what source, then, is this disastrous result to be attributed? We believe to *over-trading* both in imports and exports. Unless our merchants will put more stringent limits to their freedom of action, nothing but a *triennial* panic can keep us in check."

Now picture to yourself the French bourgeois, how in the throes of this business panic his trade-crazy brain is tortured, set in a whirl and stunned by rumours of *coups d'état* and the restoration of universal suffrage, by the struggle between parliament and the executive power, by the Fronde war between Orleanists and Legitimists, by the communist conspiracies in the south of France, by alleged *Jacqueries** in the Departments of Nièvre and Cher, by the advertisements of the different candidates for the presidency, by the cheapjack solutions offered by the journals, by the threats of the republicans to uphold the Constitution and universal suffrage by force of arms, by the gospel-preaching émigré heroes *in partibus*, who announced that the world would come to an end on the second Sunday in May 1852—think of all this and you will comprehend why in this unspeakable, deafening chaos of fusion, revision, prorogation, constitution, conspiration, coalition, emigration, usurpation and revolution, the bourgeois madly snorts at his parliamentary republic: "*Rather an end with terror than terror without end!*"

Bonaparte understood this cry. His power of comprehension was sharpened by the growing turbulence of creditors who, with each sunset which brought settling day, the second Sunday in May 1852, nearer, saw a movement of the stars protesting their earthly bills of exchange. They had become veritable astrologers. The National Assembly had blighted Bonaparte's hopes of a constitutional prolongation of his authority; the candidature of the Prince of Joinville forbade further vacillation.

If ever an event has, well in advance of its coming, cast its shadow

---

*Uprisings or revolts.

before, it was Bonaparte's *coup d'état*. As early as January 29, 1849, barely a month after his election, he had made a proposal about it to Changarnier. In the summer of 1849 his own Prime Minister, Odilon Barrot, had covertly denounced the policy of *coups d'état*; in the winter of 1850 Thiers had openly done so. In May 1851, Persigny had sought once more to win Changarnier for the *coup*; the *Messager de l'Assemblée* had published an account of these negotiations. During every parliamentary storm, the Bonapartist journals threatened a *coup d'état*, and the nearer the crisis drew, the louder grew their tone. In the orgies that Bonaparte kept up every night with men and women of the "swell mob," as soon as the hour of midnight approached and copious potations had loosened tongues and fired imaginations, the *coup d'état* was fixed for the following morning. Swords were drawn, glasses clinked, the Representatives were thrown out of the window, the imperial mantle fell upon Bonaparte's shoulders, until the following morning banished the spook once more and astonished Paris learned, from vestals of little reticence and from indiscreet paladins, of the danger it had once again escaped. During the months of September and October rumours of a *coup d'état* followed fast one after the other. Simultaneously, the shadow took on colour, like a variegated daguerreotype. Look up the September and October copies of the organs of the European daily press and you will find, word for word, intimations like the following: "Paris is full of rumours of a *coup d'état*. The capital is to be filled with troops during the night, and the next morning is to bring decrees which will dissolve the National Assembly, declare the Department of the Seine in a state of siege, restore universal suffrage and appeal to the people. Bonaparte is said to be seeking ministers for the execution of these illegal decrees." The letters that bring these tidings always end with the fateful word "*postponed*." The *coup d'état* was ever the fixed idea of Bonaparte. With this idea he had again set foot on French soil. He was so obsessed by it that he continually betrayed it and blurted it out. He was so weak that, just as continually, he gave it up again. The shadow of the *coup d'état* had become so familiar to the Parisians as a spectre that they were not willing to believe in it when it finally appeared in the flesh. What allowed the *coup d'état* to succeed was, therefore, neither the reticent reserve of the chief of the Society of December 10 nor the fact that the National Assembly was caught unawares. If it succeeded, it succeeded despite *his* indiscretion and with *its* foreknowledge, a necessary, inevitable result of antecedent developments.

On October 10 Bonaparte announced to his ministers his decision to restore universal suffrage; on the sixteenth they handed in their resignations; on the twenty-sixth Paris learned of the formation of the Thorigny ministry. Police Prefect Carlier was simultaneously replaced by Maupas; the head of the First Military Division, Magnan, concentrated the most reliable regiments in the capital. On November 4, the National Assembly resumed its sittings. It had nothing better to do than to recapitulate in a short, succinct form the course it had gone through and to prove that it was buried only after it had died.

The first post that it forfeited in the struggle with the executive power was the ministry. It had solemnly to admit this loss by accepting at full value the Thorigny ministry, a mere shadow cabinet. The Permanent Commission had received M. Giraud with laughter when he presented himself in the name of the new ministers. Such a weak ministry for such strong measures as the restoration of universal suffrage! Yet the precise object was to get nothing through *in* parliament, but everything *against* parliament.

On the very first day of its re-opening, the National Assembly received the message from Bonaparte in which he demanded the restoration of universal suffrage and the abolition of the law of May 31, 1850. The same day his ministers introduced a decree to this effect. The National Assembly at once rejected the ministry's motion of urgency and rejected the law itself on November 13 by three hundred and fifty-five votes to three hundred and forty-eight. Thus, it tore up its mandate once more; it once more confirmed the fact that it had transformed itself from the freely elected representatives of the people into the usurpatory parliament of a class; it acknowledged once more that it had itself cut in two the muscles which connected the parliamentary head with the body of the nation.

If by its motion to restore universal suffrage the executive power appealed from the National Assembly to the people, the legislative power appealed by its Quaestors' Bill from the people to the army. This Quaestors' Bill was to establish its right of directly requisitioning troops, of forming a parliamentary army. While it thus designated the army as the arbitrator between itself and the people, between itself and Bonaparte, while it recognized the army as the decisive state power, it had to confirm, on the other hand, the fact that it had long given up its claim to dominate this power. By debating its right to requisition troops, instead of requisitioning them at once, it betrayed its doubts about its own powers. By rejecting the Quaestors' Bill, it made public confession of its impotence. This bill was defeated, its proponents lacking 108 votes of a majority. The *Montagne* thus decided the issue. It found itself in the position of Buridan's ass, not, indeed, between two bundles of hay with the problem of deciding which was the more attractive, but between two showers of blows with the problem of deciding which was the harder. On the one hand, there was the fear of Changarnier; on the other, the fear of Bonaparte. It must be confessed that the position was no heroic one.

On November 18, an amendment was moved to the law on municipal elections introduced by the party of Order, to the effect that instead of three years', one year's domicile should suffice for municipal electors. The amendment was lost by a single vote, but this one vote immediately proved to be a mistake. By splitting up into its hostile factions, the party of Order had long ago forfeited its independent parliamentary majority. It showed now that there was no longer any majority at all in parliament. The National Assembly had become *incapable of transacting business*. Its atomic constituents were no longer held together by any force of cohesion; it had drawn its last breath; it was dead.

Finally, a few days before the catastrophe, the extra-parliamentary mass of the bourgeoisie was solemnly to confirm once more its breach with the bourgeoisie in parliament. Thiers, as a parliamentary hero infected more than the rest with the incurable disease of parliamentary cretinism, had, after the death of parliament, hatched out, together with the Council of State, a new parliamentary intrigue, a Responsibility Law by which the President was to be firmly held within the limits of the Constitution. Just as, on laying the foundation stone of the new market halls in Paris on September 15, Bonaparte, like a second Masaniello,* had enchanted the *dames des halles*, the fishwives—to be sure, one fishwife outweighed seventeen

---

*Tommaso Aniello (1620–1647), who went by the name Masaniello, was a Neapolitan fisherman who led a revolt of the lower classes against Spanish rule and the aristocracy.

burgraves in real power; just as after the introduction of the Quaestors' Bill he enraptured the lieutenants he regaled in the Elysée, so now, on November 25, he swept off their feet the industrial bourgeoisie, which had gathered at the circus to receive at his hands prize medals for the London Industrial Exhibition. I shall give the significant portion of his speech as reported in the *Journal des Débats*:

> "With such unhoped-for successes, I am justified in reiterating how great the French republic would be if it were permitted to pursue its real interests and reform its institutions, instead of being constantly disturbed by demagogues, on the one hand, and by monarchist hallucinations, on the other. (Loud, stormy and repeated applause from every part of the amphitheatre.) The monarchist hallucinations hinder all progress and all important branches of industry. In place of progress nothing but struggle. One sees men who were formerly the most zealous supporters of the royal authority and prerogative become partisans of a Convention merely in order to weaken the authority that has sprung from universal suffrage. (Loud and repeated applause.) We see men who have suffered most from the Revolution, and have deplored it most, provoke a new one, and merely in order to fetter the nation's will. . . . I promise you tranquillity for the future, etc., etc. (Bravo, bravo, a storm of bravos)."

Thus the industrial bourgeoisie applauds with servile bravos the *coup d'état* of December 2, the annihilation of parliament, the downfall of its own rule, the dictatorship of Bonaparte. The thunder of applause on November 25 had its answer in the thunder of cannon on December 4, and it was on the house of Monsieur Sallandrouze, who had clapped most, that they clapped most of the bombs.

Cromwell, when he dissolved the Long Parliament, went alone into its midst, drew out his watch in order that it should not continue to exist a minute after the time limit fixed by him, and drove out each one of the members of parliament with hilariously humourous taunts. Napoleon, smaller than his prototype, at least betook himself on the eighteenth Brumaire to the legislative body and read out to it, though in a faltering voice, its sentence of death. The second Bonaparte, who, moreover, found himself in possession of an executive power very different from that of Cromwell or Napoleon, sought his model not in the annals of world history, but in the annals of the Society of December 10, in the annals of the criminal courts. He robs the Bank of France of twenty-five million francs, buys General Magnan with a million, the soldiers with fifteen francs apiece and liquor, comes together with his accomplices secretly like a thief in the night, has the houses of the most dangerous parliamentary leaders broken into and Cavaignac, Lamoricière, Le Flô, Changarnier, Charras, Thiers, Baze, etc., dragged from their beds and put in prison, the chief squares of Paris and the parliamentary building occupied by troops, and cheap-Jack placards posted early in the morning on all the walls, proclaiming the dissolution of the National Assembly and the Council of State, the restoration of universal suffrage and the placing of the Seine Department in a state of siege. In like manner, he inserted a little later in the *Moniteur* a false document which asserted that influential parliamentarians had grouped themselves round him and formed a state *consulta*.*

The rump parliament, assembled in the *mairie* building† of the tenth *arrondissement* and consisting mainly of Legitimists and Orleanists, votes the deposition of Bonaparte amid repeated cries of "Long live the Republic," unavailingly harangues the gaping crowds before the building and is finally led off in the custody of African sharpshooters, first to the d'Orsay barracks, and later packed into prison vans and transported to the prisons of Mazas, Ham and Vincennes. Thus ended the party of Order, the Legislative Assembly and the February Revolution. Before hastening to close, let us briefly summarize the latter's history:

I. *First period.* From February 24 to May 4, 1848. February period. Prologue. Universal brotherhood swindle.

II. *Second period.* Period of constituting the republic and of the Constituent National Assembly.

---

*Council (Latin).
†Town hall (French).

1. May 4 to June 25, 1848. Struggle of all classes against the proletariat. Defeat of the proletariat in the June days.

2. June 25 to December 10, 1848. Dictatorship of the pure bourgeois republicans. Drafting of the Constitution. Proclamation of a state of siege in Paris. The bourgeois dictatorship set aside on December 10 by the election of Bonaparte as President.

3. December 20, 1848 to May 28, 1849. Struggle of the Constituent Assembly with Bonaparte and with the party of Order in alliance with him. Passing of the Constituent Assembly. Fall of the republican bourgeoisie.

III. *Third period.* Period of the *constitutional republic* and of the *Legislative National Assembly.*

1. May 28, 1849 to June 13, 1849. Struggle of the petty bourgeoisie with the bourgeoisie and with Bonaparte. Defeat of the petty-bourgeois democracy.

2. June 13, 1849 to May 31, 1850. Parliamentary dictatorship of the party of Order. It completes its rule by abolishing universal suffrage, but loses the parliamentary ministry.

3. May 31, 1850 to December 2, 1851. Struggle between the parliamentary bourgeoisie and Bonaparte.

   (a) May 31, 1850 to January 12, 1851. Parliament loses the supreme command of the army.

   (b) January 12 to April 11, 1851. It is worsted in its attempts to regain the administrative power. The party of Order loses its independent parliamentary majority. Its coalition with the republicans and the *Montagne.*

   (c) April 11, 1851 to October 9, 1851. Attempts at revision, fusion, prorogation. The party of Order decomposes into its separate constituents. The breach between the bourgeois parliament and press and the mass of the bourgeoisie becomes definite.

   (d) October 9 to December 2, 1851. Open breach between

parliament and the executive power. Parliament performs its dying act and succumbs, left in the lurch by its own class, by the army and by all the remaining classes. Passing of the parliamentary regime and of bourgeois rule. Victory of Bonaparte. Parody of restoration of empire.

VII

ON THE THRESHOLD OF the February Revolution, the *social republic* appeared as a phrase, as a prophecy. In the June days of 1848, it was drowned in the blood of the *Paris proletariat*, but it haunts the subsequent acts of the drama like a ghost. The *democratic republic* announces its arrival. On June 13, 1849, it is dissipated together with its *petty bourgeois*, who have taken to their heels, but in its flight it blows its own trumpet with redoubled boastfulness. The *parliamentary republic*, together with the bourgeoisie, takes possession of the entire stage; it enjoys its existence to the full, but December 2, 1851 buries it to the accompaniment of the anguished cry of the royalists in coalition: "Long live the Republic!"

The French bourgeoisie balked at the domination of the working proletariat; it has brought the *lumpenproletariat* to domination, with the chief of the Society of December 10 at the head. The bourgeoisie kept France in breathless fear of the future terrors of red anarchy; Bonaparte discounted this future for it when, on December 4, he had the eminent bourgeois of the Boulevard Montmartre and the Boulevard des Italiens shot down at their windows by the liquor-inspired army of order. It apotheosized the sword; the sword rules it. It destroyed the revolutionary press; its own press has been destroyed. It placed popular meetings under police supervision; its salons are under the supervision of the police. It disbanded the democratic National Guards; its own National Guard is disbanded. It imposed a state of siege; a state of siege is imposed upon it. It supplanted the juries by military commissions; its juries are supplanted by military commissions. It subjected public education to the sway of the priests; the priests subject it to their own education. It transported people without trial; it is being transported without trial. It repressed every stirring in society by means of the state power; every stirring in its society is suppressed by means of the state power. Out of enthusiasm for its purse, it rebelled against its own politicians and men of letters; its politicians and men of letters are swept aside, but its purse is being plundered now that its mouth has been gagged and its pen broken. The bourgeoisie never wearied of crying out to the revolution what Saint Arsenius cried out to the Christians: "*Fuge, tace, quiesce!* Flee, be silent, keep still!" Bonaparte cries to the bourgeoisie: "*Fuge, tace, quiesce!* Flee, be silent, keep still!"

The French bourgeoisie had long ago found the solution to Napoleon's dilemma: "*Dans cinquante ans l'Europe sera républicaine ou cosaque.*"* It had found the solution to it in the "*république cosaque.*" No Circe, by means of black magic, has distorted that work of art, the bourgeois republic, into a monstrous shape. That republic has lost nothing but the semblance of respectability. Present-day France was contained in a finished state within the parliamentary republic. It only required a bayonet thrust for the bubble to burst and the monster to spring forth before our eyes.

Why did the Paris proletariat not rise in revolt after December 2?

The overthrow of the bourgeoisie had as yet been only decreed; the decree had not been carried out. Any serious insurrection of the proletariat would at once have put fresh life into the bourgeoisie, would have reconciled it with the army and ensured a second June defeat for the workers.

On December 4 the proletariat was incited by bourgeois and *épicier*† to fight. On the evening of that day several legions of the National Guard promised to appear, armed and uniformed, on the scene of battle. For the bourgeois and the *épicier* had got wind of the fact that in one of his decrees of December 2 Bonaparte abolished the secret ballot and enjoined them to record their "yes" or "no" in the official registers after their names. The resistance of December 4 intimidated Bonaparte. During the night he caused placards to be posted on all the street corners of Paris, announcing the restoration of the secret ballot. The bourgeois and the *épicier* believed that they had gained their end. Those who failed to appear next morning were the bourgeois and the *épicier*.

By a *coup de main*‡ during the night of December 1 to 2, Bonaparte had robbed the Paris proletariat of its leaders, the barricade commanders. An army without officers, averse to fighting under the

---

*Within fifty years Europe will be republican or Cossack (French).
†Grocer (French).
‡Surprise attack (French).

banner of the *Montagnards* because of the memories of June 1848 and 1849 and May 1850, it left to its vanguard, the secret societies, the task of saving the insurrectionary honour of Paris, which the bourgeoisie had so unresistingly surrendered to the soldiery that, later on, Bonaparte could sneeringly give as his motive for disarming the National Guard—his fear that its arms would be turned against it itself by the anarchists!

"*C'est le triomphe complet et définitif du socialisme!*" Thus Guizot characterized December 2. But if the overthrow of the parliamentary republic contains within itself the germ of the triumph of the proletarian revolution, its immediate and palpable result was *the victory of Bonaparte over parliament, of the executive power over the legislative power, of force without phrases over the force of phrases.* In parliament the nation made its general will the law, that is, it made the law of the ruling class its general will. Before the executive power it renounces all will of its own and submits to the superior command of an alien will, to authority. The executive power, in contrast to the legislative power, expresses the heteronomy of a nation, in contrast to its autonomy. France, therefore, seems to have escaped the despotism of a class only to fall back beneath the despotism of an individual, and, what is more, beneath the authority of an individual without authority. The struggle seems to be settled in such a way that all classes, equally impotent and equally mute, fall on their knees before the rifle butt.

But the revolution is thoroughgoing. It is still journeying through purgatory. It does its work methodically. By December 2, 1851, it had completed one half of its preparatory work; it is now completing the other half. First it perfected the parliamentary power, in order to be able to overthrow it. Now that it has attained this, it perfects the *executive power*, reduces it to its purest expression, isolates it, sets it up against itself as the sole target, in order to concentrate all its forces of destruction against it. And when it has done this second half of its preliminary work, Europe will leap from its seat and exultantly exclaim: Well grubbed, old mole!*

This executive power with its enormous bureaucratic and mili-

---

*One of the many lines adapted from Shakespeare in Marx's work; this one is from Hamlet (act 1, scene 5).

tary organization, with its ingenious state machinery, embracing wide strata, with a host of officials numbering half a million, besides an army of another half million, this appalling parasitic body, which enmeshes the body of French society like a net and chokes all its pores, sprang up in the days of the absolute monarchy, with the decay of the feudal system, which it helped to hasten. The seignorial privileges of the landowners and towns became transformed into so many attributes of the state power, the feudal dignitaries into paid officials and the motley pattern of conflicting medieval plenary powers into the regulated plan of a state authority whose work is divided and centralized as in a factory. The first French Revolution, with its task of breaking all separate local, territorial, urban and provincial powers in order to create the civil unity of the nation, was bound to develop what the absolute monarchy had begun: centralization, but at the same time the extent, the attributes and the agents of governmental power. Napoleon perfected this state machinery. The Legitimist Monarchy and the July Monarchy added nothing but a greater division of labour, growing in the same measure as the division of labour within bourgeois society created new groups of interests, and, therefore, new material for state administration. Every *common* interest was straightway severed from society, counterposed to it as a higher, *general* interest, snatched from the activity of society's members themselves and made an object of government activity, from a bridge, a schoolhouse and the communal property of a village community to the railways, the national wealth and the national university of France. Finally, in its struggle against the revolution, the parliamentary republic found itself compelled to strengthen, along with the repressive measures, the resources and centralization of governmental power. All revolutions perfected this machine instead of smashing it. The parties that contended in turn for domination regarded the possession of this huge state edifice as the principal spoils of the victor.

But under the absolute monarchy, during the first Revolution, under Napoleon, bureaucracy was only the means of preparing the class rule of the bourgeoisie. Under the Restoration, under Louis Philippe, under the parliamentary republic, it was the instrument of the ruling class, however much it strove for power of its own.

Only under the second Bonaparte does the state seem to have

made itself completely independent. As against civil society, the state machine has consolidated its position so thoroughly that the chief of the Society of December 10 suffices for its head, an adventurer blown in from abroad, raised on the shield by a drunken soldiery, which he has bought with liquor and sausages, and which he must continually ply with sausage anew. Hence the downcast despair, the feeling of most dreadful humiliation and degradation that oppresses the breast of France and makes her catch her breath. She feels dishonoured.

And yet the state power is not suspended in midair. Bonaparte represents a class, and the most numerous class of French society at that, the *small-holding [Parzellen] peasants.*

Just as the Bourbons were the dynasty of big landed property and just as the Orleans were the dynasty of money, so the Bonapartes are the dynasty of the peasants, that is, the mass of the French people. Not the Bonaparte who submitted to the bourgeois parliament, but the Bonaparte who dispersed the bourgeois parliament is the chosen of the peasantry. For three years the towns had succeeded in falsifying the meaning of the election of December 10 and in cheating the peasants out of the restoration of the empire. The election of December 10, 1848, has been consummated only by the *coup d'état* of December 2, 1851.

The small-holding peasants form a vast mass, the members of which live in similar conditions but without entering into manifold relations with one another. Their mode of production isolates them from one another instead of bringing them into mutual intercourse. The isolation is increased by France's bad means of communication and by the poverty of the peasants. Their field of production, the small holding, admits of no division of labour in its cultivation, no application of science and, therefore, no diversity of development, no variety of talent, no wealth of social relationships. Each individual peasant family is almost self-sufficient; it itself directly produces the major part of its consumption and thus acquires its means of life more through exchange with nature than in intercourse with society. A small holding, a peasant and his family; alongside them another small holding, another peasant and another family. A few score of these make up a village, and a few score of villages make up a Department. In this way, the great mass of the French nation is

formed by simple addition of homologous magnitudes, much as potatoes in a sack form a sack of potatoes. In so far as millions of families live under economic conditions of existence that separate their
mode of life, their interests and their culture from those of the other
classes, and put them in hostile opposition to the latter, they form a
class. In so far as there is merely a local interconnection among these
small-holding peasants, and the identity of their interests begets no
community, no national bond and no political organization among
them, they do not form a class. They are consequently incapable of
enforcing their class interest in their own name, whether through a
parliament or through a convention. They cannot represent themselves, they must be represented. Their representative must at the
same time appear as their master, as an authority over them, as an
unlimited governmental power that protects them against the other
classes and sends them rain and sunshine from above. The political
influence of the small-holding peasants, therefore, finds its final expression in the executive power subordinating society to itself.

Historical tradition gave rise to the belief of the French peasants
in the miracle that a man named Napoleon would bring all the glory
back to them. And an individual turned up who gives himself out as
the man because he bears the name of Napoleon, in consequence of
the *Code Napoléon*,* which lays down that *la recherche de la paternité
est interdite.*† After a vagabondage of twenty years and after a series
of grotesque adventures, the legend finds fulfilment and the man becomes Emperor of the French. The fixed idea of the Nephew was realized, because it coincided with the fixed idea of the most
numerous class of the French people.

But, it may be objected, what about the peasant risings in half of
France, the raids on the peasants by the army, the mass incarceration
and transportation of peasants?

Since Louis XIV, France has experienced no similar persecution
of the peasants "on account of demagogic practices."

But let there be no misunderstanding. The Bonaparte dynasty

---

*Civil code enacted in 1804 by Napoleon to replace rule by the aristocracy with the
rule of law; it made all male citizens equals before the law and did away with hereditary nobility and class privilege.
†To research paternity is prohibited (French).

represents not the revolutionary, but the conservative peasant; not the peasant that strikes out beyond the condition of his social existence, the small holding, but rather the peasant who wants to consolidate this holding, not the country folk who, linked up with the towns, want to overthrow the old order through their own energies, but on the contrary those who, in stupefied seclusion within this old order, want to see themselves and their small holdings saved and favoured by the ghost of the empire. It represents not the enlightenment, but the superstition of the peasant; not his judgment, but his prejudice; not his future, but his past; not his modern Cevennes, but his modern Vendée.*

The three years' rigorous rule of the parliamentary republic had freed a part of the French peasants from the Napoleonic illusion and had revolutionized them, even if only superficially; but the bourgeoisie violently repressed them, as often as they set themselves in motion. Under the parliamentary republic the modern and the traditional consciousness of the French peasant contended for mastery. This progress took the form of an incessant struggle between the schoolmasters and the priests. The bourgeoisie struck down the schoolmasters. For the first time the peasants made efforts to behave independently in the face of the activity of the government. This was shown in the continual conflict between the *maires* and the prefects. The bourgeoisie deposed the *maires*. Finally, during the period of the parliamentary republic, the peasants of different localities rose against their own offspring, the army. The bourgeoisie punished them with states of siege and punitive expeditions. And this same bourgeoisie now cries out about the stupidity of the masses, the vile multitude, that has betrayed it to Bonaparte. It has itself forcibly strengthened the empire sentiments [*Imperialismus*] of the peasant class, it conserved the conditions that form the birthplace of this peasant religion. The bourgeoisie, to be sure, is bound to fear the stupidity of the masses as long as they remain conservative, and the insight of the masses as soon as they become revolutionary.

**Cévennes: region of southern France where in the early eighteenth century Protestants rebelled against King Louis XIV's attempt to impose Roman Catholicism on his subjects; *Vendée*: locale in western France and the site of counter-revolutionary insurrections during the French Revolution.

In the risings after the *coup d'état*, a part of the French peasants protested, arms in hand, against their own vote of December 10, 1848. The school they had gone through since 1848 had sharpened their wits. But they had made themselves over to the underworld of history; history held them to their word, and the majority was still so prejudiced that in precisely the reddest Departments the peasant population voted openly for Bonaparte. In its view, the National Assembly had hindered his progress. He had now merely broken the fetters that the towns had imposed on the will of the countryside. In some parts the peasants even entertained the grotesque notion of a convention side by side with Napoleon.

After the first revolution had transformed the peasants from semi-villeins into freeholders, Napoleon confirmed and regulated the conditions on which they could exploit undisturbed the soil of France which had only just fallen to their lot and slake their youthful passion for property. But what is now causing the ruin of the French peasant is his small holding itself, the division of the land, the form of property which Napoleon consolidated in France. It is precisely the material conditions which made the feudal peasant a small-holding peasant and Napoleon an emperor. Two generations have sufficed to produce the inevitable result: progressive deterioration of agriculture, progressive indebtedness of the agriculturist. The "Napoleonic" form of property, which at the beginning of the nineteenth century was the condition for the liberation and enrichment of the French country folk, has developed in the course of this century into the law of their enslavement and pauperization. And precisely this law is the first of the "*idées napoléoniennes*" which the second Bonaparte has to uphold. If he still shares with the peasants the illusion that the cause of their ruin is to be sought, not in this small-holding property itself, but outside it, in the influence of secondary circumstances, his experiments will burst like soap bubbles when they come in contact with the relations of production.

The economic development of small-holding property has radically changed the relation of the peasants to the other classes of society. Under Napoleon, the fragmentation of the land in the countryside supplemented free competition and the beginning of big industry in the towns. The peasant class was the ubiquitous protest against the landed aristocracy which had just been overthrown. The roots that small-holding property struck in French soil deprived feudalism of all nutriment. Its landmarks formed the natural fortifications of the bourgeoisie against any surprise attack on the part of its old overlords. But in the course of the nineteenth century the feudal lords were replaced by urban usurers; the feudal obligation that went with the land was replaced by the mortgage; aristocratic landed property was replaced by bourgeois capital. The small holding of the peasant is now only the pretext that allows the capitalist to draw profits, interest and rent from the soil, while leaving it to the tiller of the soil himself to see how he can extract his wages. The mortgage debt burdening the soil of France imposes on the French peasantry payment of an amount of interest equal to the annual interest on the entire British national debt. Small-holding property, in this enslavement by capital to which its development inevitably pushes forward, has transformed the mass of the French nation into troglodytes.* Sixteen million peasants (including women and children) dwell in hovels, a large number of which have but one opening, others only two and the most favoured only three. And windows are to a house what the five senses are to the head. The bourgeois order, which at the beginning of the century set the state to stand guard over the newly arisen small holding and manured it with laurels, has become a vampire that sucks out its blood and brains and throws it into the alchemistic cauldron of capital. The *Code Napoléon* is now nothing but a *codex* of distraints, forced sales and compulsory auctions. To the four million (including children, etc.) officially recognized paupers, vagabonds, criminals and prostitutes in France must be added five million who hover on the margin of existence and either have their haunts in the countryside itself or, with their rags and their children, continually desert the countryside for the towns and the towns for the countryside. The interests of the peasants, therefore, are no longer, as under Napoleon, in accord with, but in opposition to the interests of the bourgeoisie, to capital. Hence the peasants find their natural ally and leader in the *urban proletariat*, whose task is the overthrow of the bourgeois order. But *strong and unlimited government*—and this is the second "*idée napoléonienne*," which the second Napoleon has to carry out—is

---

*Cave dwellers; ignorant or reactionary persons.

called upon to defend this "material" order by force. This "*ordre matériel*" also serves as the catchword in all of Bonaparte's proclamations against the rebellious peasants.

Besides the mortgage which capital imposes on it, the small holding is burdened by *taxes*. Taxes are the source of life for the bureaucracy, the army, the priests and the court, in short, for the whole apparatus of the executive power. Strong government and heavy taxes are identical. By its very nature, small-holding property forms a suitable basis for an all-powerful and innumerable bureaucracy. It creates a uniform level of relationships and persons over the whole surface of the land. Hence it also permits of uniform action from a supreme centre on all points of this uniform mass. It annihilates the aristocratic intermediate grades between the mass of the people and the state power. On all sides, therefore, it calls forth the direct interference of this state power and the interposition of its immediate organs. Finally, it produces an unemployed surplus population for which there is no place either on the land or in the towns, and which accordingly reaches out for state offices as a sort of respectable alms, and provokes the creation of state posts. By the new markets which he opened at the point of the bayonet, by the plundering of the Continent, Napoleon repaid the compulsory taxes with interest. These taxes were a spur to the industry of the peasant, whereas now they rob his industry of its last resources and complete his inability to resist pauperism. And an enormous bureaucracy, well-gallooned and well-fed, is the "*idée napaléonienne*" which is most congenial of all to the second Bonaparte. How could it be otherwise, seeing that alongside the actual classes of society he is forced to create an artificial caste, for which the maintenance of his regime becomes a bread-and-butter question? Accordingly, one of his first financial operations was the raising of officials' salaries to their old level and the creation of new sinecures.

Another "*idée napoléonienne*" is the domination of the *priests* as an instrument of government. But while in its accord with society, in its dependence on natural forces and its submission to the authority which protected it from above, the small holding that had newly come into being was naturally religious, the small holding that is ruined by debts, at odds with society and authority, and driven beyond its own limitations naturally becomes irreligious.

Heaven was quite a pleasing accession to the narrow strip of land just won, more particularly as it makes the weather; it becomes an insult as soon as it is thrust forward as substitute for the small holding. The priest then appears as only the anointed bloodhound of the earthly police—another "*idée napoléonienne*." On the next occasion, the expedition against Rome will take place in France itself, but in a sense opposite to that of M. de Montalembert.*

Lastly, the culminating point of the "*idées napoléoniennes*" is the preponderance of the *army*. The army was the *point d'honneur* of the small-holding peasants, it was they themselves transformed into heroes, defending their new possessions against the outer world, glorifying their recently won nationhood, plundering and revolutionizing the world. The uniform was their own state dress; war was their poetry; the small holding, extended and rounded off in imagination, was their fatherland, and patriotism the ideal form of the sense of property. But the enemies against whom the French peasant has now to defend his property are not the Cossacks; they are the *huissiers*† and the tax collectors. The small holding lies no longer in the so-called fatherland, but in the register of mortgages. The army itself is no longer the flower of the peasant youth; it is the swamp-flower of the peasant *lumpenproletariat*. It consists in large measure of *remplaçants*, of substitutes, just as the second Bonaparte is himself only a *remplaçant*, the substitute for Napoleon. It now performs its deeds of valour by hounding the peasants in masses like chamois,‡ by doing *gendarme* duty, and if the internal contradictions of his system chase the chief of the Society of December 10 over the French border, his army, after some acts of brigandage, will reap, not laurels, but thrashings.

One sees: *all* "idées napoléoniennes" *are ideas of the undeveloped small holding in the freshness of its youth*; for the small holding that has outlived its day they are an absurdity. They are only the hallucinations of its death struggle, words that are transformed into phrases, spirits transformed into ghosts. But the parody of the em-

---

*Charles René Forbes Montalembert (1810–1870), historian and leader of liberal Roman Catholics during the July Monarchy (see footnote on p. 70).
†Bailiffs (French).
‡Horned and hoofed goat-like animals prized for their meat and pliant skin.

pire [*des Imperialismus*] was necessary to free the mass of the French nation from the weight of tradition and to work out in pure form the opposition between the state power and society. With the progressive undermining of small-holding property, the state structure erected upon it collapses. The centralization of the state that modern society requires arises only on the ruins of the military-bureaucratic government machinery which was forged in opposition to feudalism.

The condition of the French peasants provides us with the answer to the riddle of the *general elections of December 20 and 21,* which bore the second Bonaparte up Mount Sinai, not to receive laws, but to give them.

Manifestly, the bourgeoisie had now no choice but to elect Bonaparte. When the puritans at the Council of Constance* complained of the dissolute lives of the popes and wailed about the necessity of moral reform, Cardinal Pierre d'Ailly thundered at them: "Only the devil in person can still save the Catholic Church, and you ask for angels." In like manner, after the *coup d'état,* the French bourgeoisie cried: Only the chief of the Society of December 10 can still save bourgeois society! Only theft can still save property; only perjury, religion; bastardy, the family; disorder, order!

As the executive authority which has made itself an independent power, Bonaparte feels it to be his mission to safeguard "bourgeois order." But the strength of this bourgeois order lies in the middle class. He looks on himself, therefore, as the representative of the middle class and issues decrees in this sense. Nevertheless, he is somebody solely due to the fact that he has broken the political power of this middle class and daily breaks it anew. Consequently, he looks on himself as the adversary of the political and literary power of the middle class. But by protecting its material power, he generates its political power anew. The cause must accordingly be kept alive; but the effect, where it manifests itself, must be done away with. But this cannot pass off without slight confusions of cause and effect, since in their interaction both lose their distinguishing features. New decrees that obliterate the border line. As

---

*Roman Catholic council held from 1414 to 1418 in Constance, Germany, to resolve the schism created by the existence of three rival popes.

against the bourgeoisie, Bonaparte looks on himself, at the same time, as the representative of the peasants and of the people in general, who wants to make the lower classes of the people happy within the frame of bourgeois society. New decrees that cheat the "True Socialists"* of their statecraft in advance. But, above all, Bonaparte looks on himself as the chief of the Society of December 10, as the representative of the *lumpenproletariat* to which he himself, his *entourage*, his government and his army belong, and whose prime consideration is to benefit itself and draw California lottery prizes from the state treasury. And he vindicates his position as chief of the Society of December 10 with decrees, without decrees and despite decrees.

This contradictory task of the man explains the contradictions of his government, the confused groping about which seeks now to win, now to humiliate first one class and then another and arrays all of them uniformly against him, whose practical uncertainty forms a highly comical contrast to the imperious, categorical style of the government decrees, a style which is faithfully copied from the Uncle.

Industry and trade, hence the business affairs of the middle class, are to prosper in hothouse fashion under the strong government. The grant of innumerable railway concessions. But the Bonapartist *lumpenproletariat* is to enrich itself. The initiated play *tripotage*† on the *bourse* with the railway concessions. But no capital is forthcoming for the railways. Obligation of the Bank to make advances on railway shares. But, at the same time, the Bank is to be exploited for personal ends and therefore must be cajoled. Release of the Bank from the obligation to publish its report weekly. Leonine agreement of the Bank with the government. The people are to be given employment. Initiation of public works. But the public works increase the obligations of the people in respect of taxes. Hence reduction of the taxes by an onslaught on the *rentiers*,‡ by conversion of the five per cent bonds to four-and-a-half per cent. But, once more, the middle class must receive a

---

*Name given by Marx to a particular brand of idealizing and weak socialists; also see *Manifesto of the Communist Party*, pp. 32ff.

† *Tripotage*: hanky-panky; *bourse*: stock exchange (French).

‡Those who live on the proceeds of investments.

*douceur.** Therefore doubling of the wine tax for the people, who buy it *en détail,* and halving of the wine tax for the middle class, who drink it *en gros.* Dissolution of the actual workers' associations, but promises of miracles of association in the future. The peasants are to be helped. Mortgage banks that expedite their getting into debt and accelerate the concentration of property. But these banks are to be used to make money out of the confiscated estates of the House of Orleans. No capitalist wants to agree to this condition, which is not in the decree, and the mortgage bank remains a mere decree, etc., etc.

Bonaparte would like to appear as the patriarchal benefactor of all classes. But he cannot give to one class without taking from another. Just as at the time of the Fronde it was said of the Duke of Guise that he was the most *obligeant*† man in France because he had turned all his estates into his partisans' obligations to him, so Bonaparte would fain be the most *obligeant* man in France and turn all the property, all the labour of France into a personal obligation to himself. He would like to steal the whole of France in order to be able to make a present of her to France or, rather, in order to be able to buy France anew with French money, for as the chief of the Society of December 10 he must needs buy what ought to belong to him. And all the state institutions, the Senate, the Council of State, the legislative body, the Legion of Honour, the soldiers' medals, the washhouses, the public works, the railways, the *état major*‡ of the National Guard to the exclusion of privates, and the confiscated estates of the House of Orleans—all become parts of the institution of purchase. Every place in the army and in the government machine becomes a means of purchase. But the most important feature of this process, whereby France is taken in order to give to her, is the percentages that find their way into the pockets of the head and the members of the Society of December 10 during the turnover. The witticism with which Countess L., the mistress of M. de Morny, characterized the confiscation of the Orleans estates: *"C'est le premier vol de l'aigle"*§ is applicable to every flight of this

---

*Douceur: a sop or gesture of appeasement; *en détail:* retail; *en gros:* in bulk (French).
†Obliging (French).
‡General Staff (French).
§*Vol* means flights and theft [Marx's note]. *De l'aigle:* of the eagle (French).

eagle, which is more like a *raven*. He himself and his adherents call out to one another daily like that Italian Carthusian admonishing the miser who, with boastful display, counted up the goods on which he could yet live for years to come: "*Tu fai conto sopra i beni, bisogna prima far il conto sopra gil anni.*"* Lest they make a mistake in the years, they count the minutes. A bunch of blokes push their way forward to the court, into the ministries, to the head of the administration and the army, a crowd of the best of whom it must be said that no one knows whence he comes, a noisy, disreputable, rapacious bohème that crawls into gallooned coats with the same grotesque dignity as the high dignitaries of Soulouque. One can visualize clearly this upper stratum of the Society of December 10, if one reflects that *Véron-Crevel*† is its preacher of morals and *Granier de Cassagnac* its thinker. When Guizot, at the time of his ministry, utilized this Granier on a hole-and-corner newspaper against the dynastic opposition, he used to boast of him with the quip: "*C'est le roi des drôles*," "he is the king of buffoons." One would do wrong to recall the Regency or Louis XV in connection with Louis Bonaparte's court and clique. For "often already, France has experienced a government of mistresses; but never before a government of *hommes entretenus.*"‡

Driven by the contradictory demands of his situation and being at the same time, like a conjurer, under the necessity of keeping the public gaze fixed on himself, as Napoleon's substitute, by springing constant surprises, that is to say, under the necessity of executing a *coup d'état en miniature* every day, Bonaparte throws the entire bourgeois economy into confusion, violates everything that seemed inviolable to the Revolution of 1848, makes some tolerant of revolution, others desirous of revolution, and produces actual anarchy in the name of order, while at the same time stripping its halo from the entire state machine, profanes it and makes it at once loathsome and

---

*"Thou countest thy goods, thou shouldst first count thy years" [Marx's note].

†In his work, *Cousine Bette*, Balzac delineates the thoroughly dissolute Parisian philistine in Crevel, a character which he draws after the model of Dr. Véron, the proprietor of the *Constitutionnel* [Marx's note].

‡The words quoted are those of Madame Girardin [Marx's note]. *Hommes entretenus*: gigolos (French).

ridiculous. The cult of the Holy Tunic of Treves* he duplicates at Paris in the cult of the Napoleonic imperial mantle. But when the imperial mantle finally falls on the shoulders of Louis Bonaparte, the bronze statue of Napoleon will crash from the top of the Vendôme Column.

---

*Seamless outer garment that some believe Jesus Christ wore; kept in the Cathedral of Trèves, in Germany.

PREFACES to THE EIGHTEENTH BRUMAIRE OF LOUIS BONAPARTE

Karl Marx
Friedrich Engels

Marx's Preface to the Second Edition

My friend *Joseph Weydemeyer*,* whose death was so untimely, intended to publish a political weekly in New York starting from January 1, 1852. He invited me to provide this weekly with a history of the *coup d'état*. Down to the middle of February, I accordingly wrote him weekly articles under the title: *The Eighteenth Brumaire of Louis Bonaparte*. Meanwhile Weydemeyer's original plan had fallen through. Instead, in the spring of 1852 he began to publish a monthly, *Die Revolution*, the first number of which consists of my *Eighteenth Brumaire*. A few hundred copies of this found their way into Germany at that time, without, however, getting into the actual book trade. A German bookseller of extremely radical pretensions to whom I offered the sale of my book was most virtuously horrified at a "presumption" so "contrary to the times."

From the above facts it will be seen that the present work took shape under the immediate pressure of events and its historical material does not extend beyond the month of February (1852). Its republication now is due in part to the demand of the book trade, in part to the urgent requests of my friends in Germany.

Of the writings dealing with the same subject approximately *at the same time* as mine, only two deserve notice: Victor Hugo's *Napoléon le Petit* [*Napoleon the Little*] and Proudhon's *Coup d'Etat*.

Victor Hugo confines himself to bitter and witty invective against the responsible publisher of the *coup d'état*. The event itself appears in his work like a bolt from the blue. He sees in it only the violent act of a single individual. He does not notice that he makes this individual great instead of little by ascribing to him a personal power of initiative such as would be without parallel in world history. Proudhon, for his part, seeks to represent the *coup d'état* as the result of an antecedent historical development. Unnoticeably, however, his historical construction of the *coup d'état* becomes a historical *apologia* for its hero. Thus he falls into the error of our so-called *objective* historians. I, on the contrary, demonstrate how the *class struggle* in France created circumstances and relationships that made it possible for a grotesque mediocrity to play a hero's part.

---

*Military commandant of the St. Louis district during the American Civil War [Marx's note].

A revision of the present work would have robbed it of its peculiar colouring. Accordingly I have confined myself to mere correction of printer's errors and to striking out allusions now no longer intelligible.

The concluding words of my work: "But when the imperial mantle finally falls on the shoulders of Louis Bonaparte, the bronze statue of Napoleon will crash from the top of the Vendôme Column," have already been fulfilled.

Colonel Charras opened the attack on the Napoleon cult in his work on the campaign of 1815. Subsequently, and particularly in the last few years, French literature made an end of the Napoleon legend with the weapons of historical research, of criticism, of satire and of wit. Outside France this violent breach with the traditional popular belief, this tremendous mental revolution, has been little noticed and still less understood.

Lastly, I hope that my work will contribute towards eliminating the school-taught phrase now current, particularly in Germany, of so-called *Caesarism*. In this superficial historical analogy the main point is forgotten, namely, that in ancient Rome the class struggle took place only within a privileged minority, between the free rich and the free poor, while the great productive mass of the population, the slaves, formed the purely passive pedestal for these combatants. People forget *Sismondi's* significant saying: The Roman proletariat lived at the expense of society, while modern society lives at the expense of the proletariat. With so complete a difference between the material, economic conditions of the ancient and the modern class struggles, the political figures produced by them can likewise have no more in common with one another than the Archbishop of Canterbury has with the High Priest Samuel.

London, June 23, 1869
KARL MARX

F. Engels's Preface to the Third German Edition

The fact that a new edition of *The Eighteenth Brumaire* has become necessary, thirty-three years after its first appearance, proves that even today this little book has lost none of its value.

It was in truth a work of genius. Immediately after the event that struck the whole political world like a thunderbolt from the blue, that was condemned by some with loud cries of moral indignation and accepted by others as salvation from the revolution and as punishment for its errors, but was only wondered at by all and understood by none—immediately after this event Marx came out with a concise, epigrammatic exposition that laid bare the whole course of French history since the February days in its inner interconnection, reduced the miracle of December 2 to a natural, necessary result of this interconnection and in so doing did not even need to treat the hero of the *coup d'état* otherwise than with the contempt he so well deserved. And the picture was drawn with such a master hand that every fresh disclosure since made has only provided fresh proofs of how faithfully it reflected reality. This eminent understanding of the living history of the day, this clear-sighted appreciation of events at the moment of happening, is indeed without parallel.

But for this, Marx's thorough knowledge of French history was needed. France is the land where, more than anywhere else, the historical class struggles were each time fought out to a decision, and where, consequently, the changing political forms within which they move and in which their results are summarized have been stamped in the sharpest outlines. The centre of feudalism in the Middle Ages, the model country of unified monarchy, resting on estates, since the Renaissance, France demolished feudalism in the Great Revolution and established the unalloyed rule of the bourgeoisie in a classical purity unequalled by any other European land. And the struggle of the upward-striving proletariat against the ruling bourgeoisie appeared here in an acute form unknown elsewhere. This was the reason why Marx not only studied the past history of France with particular predilection, but also followed her current history in every detail, stored up the material for future use and, consequently, events never took him by surprise.

In addition, however, there was still another circumstance. It was precisely Marx who had first discovered the great law of motion of history, the law according to which all historical struggles, whether they proceed in the political, religious, philosophical or some other ideological domain, are in fact only the more or less clear expression of struggles of social classes, and that the existence and thereby the collisions, too, between these classes are in turn conditioned by the degree of development of their economic position, by the mode of their production and of their exchange determined by it. This law, which has the same significance for history as the law of the transformation of energy has for natural science—this law gave him here, too, the key to an understanding of the history of the Second French Republic. He put his law to the test on these historical events, and even after thirty-three years we must still say that it has stood the test brilliantly.

Hamburg, 1885
FRIEDERICK ENGELS

THESES ON FEUERBACH

KARL MARX
(slightly revised by Friedrich Engels)
translated by Martin Puchner

1. The main flaw of all previous materialisms—that of Feuerbach*
   included—is that the object, reality, and sensuousness are understood only in terms of the *object* or of *its being contemplated*;
   but not in terms of sensuous, human activity, of practice, not
   subjectively. For this reason it so happened that the *active* part
   was developed by idealism, rather than by materialism, but only
   in an abstract manner, since idealism naturally does not fully
   recognize real, sensuous activity. Feuerbach does want sensuous
   objects that are different from objects of thought, but he does
   not understand human activity as itself an objective activity. In
   The Essence of Christianity he therefore considers only theoretical activities as essentially human, while he grasps and identifies
   practice only in its "dirty-Jewish" manifestation. He thus does
   not understand the significance of "revolutionary," of practical-
   critical activity.

2. The question whether we can attribute objective truth to human
   thought is not a theoretical question but a practical question.
   Man must prove the truth, i.e. the reality and power, the world-
   liness of his thinking, in practice. The debate about the reality
   and unreality of thought, once it is isolated from practice, is a
   purely *scholastic* question.

3. The materialist doctrine—that humans are the product of circumstances and education and that changed humans are thus
   the product of changed circumstances and education—forgets
   that circumstances are changed by humans and that the educator himself must be educated. It must therefore split society into
   two parts—of which one is elevated above society (for example
   in Robert Owen).†

   The convergence of the changing of circumstances and of
   human action can only be understood and comprehended ra-
   tionally as *revolutionary practice*.

---

*Ludwig Andreas Feuerbach (1804–1872), German philosopher who sought to ex-
plain the world of ideas, including religion and philosophy, by relating them to the
material circumstances from which they arose. His most famous sentence inverts
Genesis 1:27: "Man created God after his own image."
†Robert Owen (1771–1858), British socialist, economist, and industrialist who created new communities of living and working based on his theories of labor and
shared possession of the means of production.

4. Feuerbach takes his point of departure from the fact of religious self-alienation, from the doubling of the world into a religious, imagined world and a real world. His work consists of reducing the religious world to its secular foundation. He does not see that after completing this work the main thing still remains to be done. The fact that the secular foundation splits in two and creates a separate realm in the clouds can only be explained by the fact that the secular foundation is torn apart and in contradiction with itself. This contradiction within the foundation must first be comprehended and then, by eliminating the contradiction, revolutionized. For example, after the human family has been shown to be the secret of the holy family, the former must then be theoretically and practically transformed.

5. Not content with abstract thought, Feuerbach appeals to the contemplation of the sensuous world, but he does not understand sensuousness to be the *practical* activity of humans using their senses.

6. Feuerbach reduces religious essence to human essence. But human essence is not an abstract notion inherent in the isolated individual. In reality, it is the ensemble of social relations. Feuerbach, who does not critique this reality, is therefore forced

    1. to abstract from the historical process and to create a religious sentiment that exists by itself and to assume a human individual that is abstract and isolated.

    2. to comprehend essence only as "species," as an inherent, tacit generality that connects all the individuals in a *natural* manner.

7. For this reason, Feuerbach does not see that the "religious sentiment" is itself a social product and that the abstract individual whom he analyzes belongs to a particular form of society.

8. Social life is essentially *practical*. All mysteries that mislead theory to mysticism find their rational solution in human practice and in the comprehension of this practice.

9. The highest achievement of contemplative materialism, i.e. a

materialism that does not understand sensuousness as practical activity, is the contemplation of isolated individuals in bourgeois society.

10. The standpoint of the old materialism is bourgeois society, the standpoint of the new materialism is human society or socialized humanity.

11. Philosophers have merely *interpreted* the world in different ways; but the point is to *change* it.

Comments & Questions

In this section, we aim to provide the reader with an array of perspectives on the text, as well as questions that challenge those perspectives. The commentary has been culled from sources as diverse as reviews contemporaneous with the work, letters written by the author, literary criticism of later generations, and appreciations written throughout the work's history. Following the commentary, a series of questions seeks to filter Karl Marx and Friederick Engels's The Communist Manifesto and Other Writings *through a variety of points of view and bring about a richer understanding of these enduring works.*

Comments

NEW YORK SUN

Karl Marx was not only a vigorous and fruitful thinker—the strongest, best equipped, and most accomplished intellect which has ever approached the labor problem from a workman's point of view—but he has been for nearly half a century the standard bearer and organizer of the great labor movement whose principles and programme he has formulated. It is true that the International Society which he founded and for some time personally directed has been virtually broken up, but the habit of cooperative effort which he instilled has transformed the laboring masses throughout Europe into a coherent, resolute, and mighty social force. They to whom his life was devoted are not likely to forget the watchword in which he summed up the lessons of experience and pointed out the harsh remedy. "Proletarians," he said, "have nothing to lose but their chains. They have a world to win. Let, therefore, the proletarians of all countries combine with one another!"

—March 16, 1883

FRIEDRICH ENGELS

Just as Darwin discovered the law of development of organic nature, so Marx discovered the law of development of human history: the simple fact, hitherto concealed by an overgrowth of ideology, that mankind must first of all eat, drink, have shelter and clothing, before it can pursue politics, science, art, religion, etc.; that therefore the production of the immediate material means of subsistence and consequently the degree of economic development attained by a given people or during a given epoch form the foundation upon which the state institutions, the legal conceptions, art, and even the ideas on religion, of the people concerned have been evolved, and in the light of which they must, therefore, be explained, instead of *vice versa*, as had hitherto been the case.

But that is not all. Marx also discovered the special law of motion governing the present-day capitalist mode of production and the bourgeois society that this mode of production has created. The discovery of surplus value suddenly threw light on the problem, in trying to solve which all previous investigations, of both bourgeois economists and socialist critics, had been groping in the dark.

—from "Speech at the Graveside of Karl Marx" (March 17, 1883); reprinted in *The Marx-Engels Reader* (1972)

ELEANOR MARX (KARL MARX'S DAUGHTER)

In 1847 . . . Marx founded a German Working-Man's Club at Brussels, and, what is of more importance, joined, together with his political friends, the 'Communist League.' The whole organization of the League was changed by him; from a hole-and-corner conspiracy it was transformed into an organization for the propaganda of Communist principles, and was only secret because existing circumstances made secrecy a necessity. Wherever German working-men's clubs existed the League existed also, and it was the first socialist movement of an international character, Englishmen, Belgians, Hungarians, Poles, Scandinavians being members; it was the first organization of the Social Democratic Party. In 1847 a Congress of the League was held in London, at which Marx and Engels assisted as delegates; and they were subsequently appointed to write the celebrated 'Manifesto of the Communist Party'—first published just before the Revolution of 1848, and then translated into well nigh all European languages. This Manifesto opens with a review of the existing conditions of society. It goes on to show how gradually the old feudal division of classes has disappeared, and how modern society is divided simply into two classes—that of the capitalist or bourgeois class, and that of the proletariat; of the expropriators and expropriated; of the bourgeois class possessing wealth and power and producing nothing. The bourgeoisie, after using the proletariat to fight its political battles against feudalism, has used the power thus acquired to enslave the proletariat. To the charge that Communism aims at 'abolishing property,' the Manifesto replied that Communists aim only at abolishing the bourgeois system of property, by which already for nine-tenths of the community property is abolished; to the accusation that Communists aim at 'abolishing marriage and the family,' the Manifesto answered by asking what kind of 'family' and 'marriage' were possible for the working men, for whom in all true meaning of the words neither exists. As to 'abolishing fatherland and nationality,' these are abolished for the proletariat, and, thanks to the development of industry, for the bourgeoisie also. The bourgeoisie has wrought great revolutions in history; it has revolutionised the whole system of production. Under its hands the steam-engine, the self-acting mule, the steam-hammer, the railways and ocean-steamers of our days were developed. But its most revolutionary production was the production of the proletariat, of a class whose very conditions of existence compel it to overthrow the whole actual society.

—from *Progress* (May 1883)

EDWARD AVELING

The most impressive personalities I have ever met were Karl Marx, Charles Darwin, Frederick Engels, and, in quite another direction of life, Henry Irving.

—from *The Labour Prophet* (1895)

JOHN SPARGO

It is quite remarkable that practically all socialists, whether they be opportunists or impossibilists, proletarians or intellectuals, or even anti-intellectuals, claim to be 'Marxists.' The English socialist who works with the trade unionist, through the Labor Party, claims to be a pure Marxist. The same claim is made by the impatient 'syndicalist' of the Latin countries, with his faith in the mass strike and his ill-concealed disdain for parliamentary action. In practically all

socialist factional discussions Marx is the prophet of all the factions. . . .

'As for me, I am no "Marxist," I am glad to say,' was a saying frequently upon the lips of Marx. With the words went that half-sneering
expression with which his best portraits have made us familiar. If we
can fathom the meaning of the cryptic and paradoxical utterance, it
may assist us very materially in our attempt to find a satisfactory answer to our question. Who, then, were the 'Marxists' thus scornfully repudiated by Marx, and what were the reasons for the repudiation?

During his lifetime, as now, there were many disciples of Marx
who regarded his theoretical work as being his greatest achievement,
and his most important contribution to the cause of the proletariat.
He was to them primarily a political economist. They spoke of his
great work, *Das Kapital,* as the 'Bible of the proletariat,' and as a Bible
they regarded it. With a passion which can only be adequately described as religious, tens of thousands of working-men laboriously
read and studied that difficult work. It was to them an 'impregnable
rock of Holy Scripture.' Those who could not comprehend the work
as a whole satisfied themselves with a few memorized passages. Like
all Bibles, it became a book of texts, much quoted but little read.

Naturally, those who regarded the book as a Bible made it the
basis of a creed. Naturally, also, their creed became the basis of a sect.
Doctrinal tests decided the fitness or unfitness of men and women
to enter the socialist fellowship and to be reckoned with the elect.
Just as religious sectarianism based upon creedal and doctrinal tests
has barred many a rare and beautiful religious spirit from the
church, while it placed the word 'orthodox' as a stamp of approval
upon many an unworthy and irreligious spirit, so this sectarian
'Marxism' imposed its stamp of 'orthodox' and 'unorthodox' to determine the fitness or unfitness of men and women to be called socialists. Many who believed in the whole program of socialism, who
saw the necessity of a working-class political party to bring about
the realization of that program, and were willing to work with and
through such a party for the immediate interests of the working-
class, and, ultimately, the collective ownership of the social productive forces, were denied the right to call themselves socialists, and a
place in the socialist ranks, simply because they could not subscribe
to all the economic and philosophical teachings of Marx. . . .

In the *Communist Manifesto*, that work which may be said to be the corner-stone of modern scientific socialism, we find him laying emphasis upon the fact that the transformation which he calls the social revolution is not to be a sudden act. He speaks of the 'first step in the revolution' being the struggle for political democracy, the attainment of the franchise by the proletariat. That accomplished, the proletariat is to wrest, 'by degrees,' the control of the social productive forces from the hated *bourgeoisie*. His insistence upon the necessity of a 'first step,' and of a conquest of the economic resources 'by degrees,' shows very clearly that, from the first, Marx repudiated the old notion of sudden, catastrophic revolution. His ideal was one of the 'revolutionary evolution.'

In the same profound and epoch-making pamphlet Marx lays stress upon the fact that the socialists, because they accept the class struggle as their fundamental and guiding philosophy, must not confine themselves to working for the attainment of the ultimate interest of the proletariat, the abolition of wage-labor and its inevitable exploitation and oppression, but own the 'momentary interests' of the workers as well as their ultimate aim. In pursuance of that thought he outlined a program of social reform upon which socialists and progressive social reformers are making common cause today in every country where the socialist parties are represented in the legislatures.

—from the *American Journal of Sociology* (1911)

V. I. LENIN

Marxism is the system of Marx's views and teachings. Marx was the genius who continued and consummated the three main ideological currents of the nineteenth century, as represented by the three most advanced countries of mankind: classical German philosophy, classical English political economy, and French socialism combined with French revolutionary doctrines in general. Acknowledged even by his opponents, the remarkable consistency and integrity of Marx's views [constitute] modern materialism and modern scientific socialism, as the theory and programme of the working-class movement in all the civilised countries of the world.

—from *Selected Works in Three Volumes* (1916)

HANNAH ARENDT

Our tradition of political thought had its definite beginning in the teachings of Plato and Aristotle. I believe it came to a no less definite end in the theories of Karl Marx.

—from *Between Past and Future* (1961)

Questions

1. What do you think of Marx's dictum that history repeats itself, the second time as farce? Has any recent event of historical importance repeated a prior one, but as farce? If America were to have another revolution, would it be farcical?

2. Is there any sign that the American proletariat is revolutionary? Do you know of any successful Marxist revolution that was led by the proletariat?

3. Do you think that the passage in which Marx argues that the bourgeoisie has destroyed all venerable prejudices and unsettled all traditional relations so that "all that is solid melts into air" (see page 10) contains a note of nostalgia, even of conservatism? Is Marxism in part an attempt to restore something lost?

4. The socialist Soviet Union is no more; China is gradually shifting away from pure Marxism; North Korea is in economic trouble. Does the failure of Marxist nations discredit Marxism?

For Further Reading

The Life and Works of Karl Marx

Althusser, Louis. *For Marx.* Translated by Ben Brewster. London: Verso, 1996.

Berlin, Isaiah. *Karl Marx: His Life and Environment.* 1939. London: Oxford University Press, 1982.

Berman, Marshall. *All That Is Solid Melts into Air: The Experience of Modernity.* London: Penguin, 1988.

Dupré, Louis Karel. *The Philosophical Foundations of Marxism.* New York: Harcourt, Brace and World, 1966.

Harries, Martin. *Scare Quotes from Shakespeare: Marx, Keynes, and the Language of Reenchantment.* Stanford, CA: Stanford University Press, 2000.

Fedoseyev, P. N., et al. *Karl Marx: A Biography.* Prepared by the Institute of Marxism-Leninism of the Communist Party of the Soviet Union (CPSU) Central Committee. Translated by Yuri Sdobinkov. Moscow: Progress Publishers, 1973.

History

Hobsbawm, Eric J. *The Age of Revolution: Europe 1789–1848.* Cleveland, OH: World Publishing Company, 1962.

———. *Age of Capital: 1848–1875.* New York: Charles Scribner's Sons, 1975.

Sassoon, Donald. *One Hundred Years of Socialism: The West European Left in the Twentieth Century.* New York: The New Press, 1996.

Examples of Marxian Criticism

Anderson, Perry. "Modernity and Revolution." In *Marxism and the Interpretation of Culture,* edited and with an introduction by Cary Nelson and Lawrence Grossberg. Urbana: University of Illinois Press, 1988.

Derrida, Jacques. *Specters of Marx: The State of the Debt, the Work of*

Mourning, and the New International. Translated by Peggy Kamuf. New York: Routledge, 1994.

Hardt, Michael, and Antonio Negri. *Empire.* Cambridge, MA: Harvard University Press, 2001.

Harvey, David. *Spaces of Capital: Towards a Critical Geography.* New York: Routledge, 2001.

Jameson, Fredric. *Marxism and Form: Twentieth-Century Dialectical Theories of Literature.* Princeton, NJ: Princeton University Press, 1971.

Laclau, Ernesto. *New Reflections on the Revolution of Our Time.* London: Verso, 1990.

Spivak, Gayatri Chakravorty. "Can the Subaltern Speak?" In *Marxism and the Interpretation of Culture,* edited and with an introduction by Cary Nelson and Lawrence Grossberg. Urbana: University of Illinois Press, 1988.

Williams, Raymond. *Marxism and Literature.* Oxford: Oxford University Press, 1977.